THE GREATEST INTERGALACTIC GUIDE TO SPACE EVER

by the Brainwaves

Illustrated by Lisa Swerling and Ralph Lazar   Written by Carole Stott

FINISH

DK

London, New York, Melbourne,
Munich, and Delhi

Senior Editor Andrea Mills
Senior Art Editor Jim Green
Editor Steven Carton
Designer Katie Knutton

Managing Editor Linda Esposito
Managing Art Editor Diane Thistlethwaite

Consultant Jacqueline Mitton

Publishing Manager Andrew Macintyre
Category Publisher Laura Buller

Production Editor Melissa Latorre
Senior Production Controller Angela Graef

Jacket Copywriter Adam Powley
Jacket Editor Mariza O'Keeffe

First published in Great Britain in 2009
by Dorling Kindersley Limited,
80 Strand, London WC2R 0RL

Colour reproduction by
Media Development Printing Ltd.

Printed and bound by LEO, China

Discover more at
www.dk.com
www.thebrainwaves.com

Look out for me!

I'm Sidney Spacehopper and my
bounce is as big as my waistline. I'll be
munching my way through the book,
filling up with Space junk and inflating
as I go. Wait until you see me at the
end of the book – I'm bursting to tell
you, but it's a Space-tacular surprise!

CONTENTS

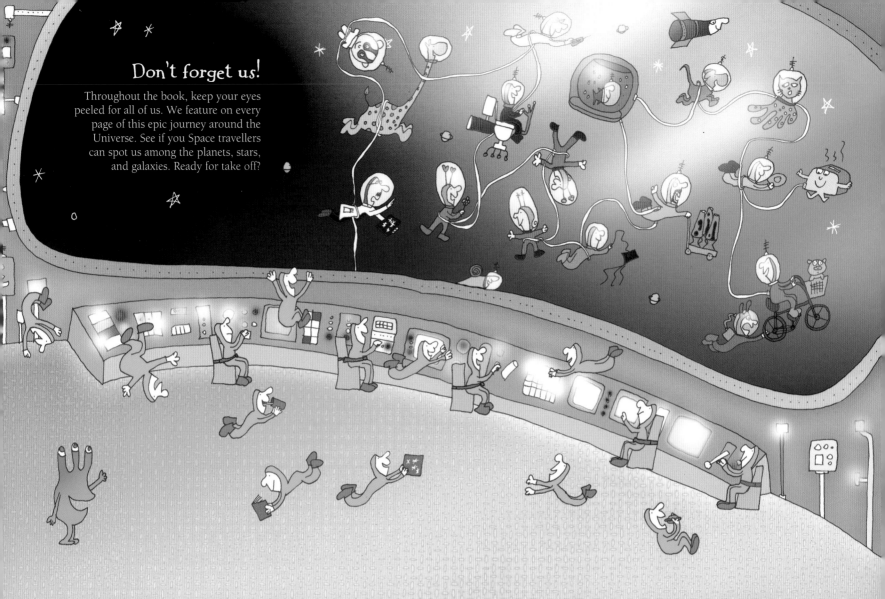

Don't forget us!

Throughout the book, keep your eyes peeled for all of us. We feature on every page of this epic journey around the Universe. See if you Space travellers can spot us among the planets, stars, and galaxies. Ready for take off?

COSMIC ZOO

The Universe is a vast expanse made up of everything that we know about, as well as everything that we have left to discover. It includes all that we can see with our eyes, as well as material and energy that we detect in other ways. The range of objects in the Universe is diverse. At first, they may appear unrelated, but these objects are grouped into types and share a common history.

Planetary worlds

Our home in the Universe is planet Earth. It feels large and special to us, and was once believed to be the centre of the Universe. Today, it is known to be relatively tiny and one of many planets.

Solar System planets

Eight planets, including Earth, and many smaller objects orbit the Sun. They are jointly known as the Solar System. Though the planets formed together, they are very different. Earth is third from the Sun and fifth largest.

Dwarf planets

Small planet-like objects known as dwarf planets exist in the Solar System. They are almost round in shape and orbit the Sun in a region occupied by even smaller objects.

Planetary remains

Not all of the material that produced the Solar System planets was used up in the process. Asteroids, Kuiper Belt Objects, and comets, which inhabit different parts of the system, are all unused material.

Planetary moons

Six of the Solar System planets have moons orbiting around them. Between them they share more than 160. The biggest moon is larger than the smallest planet, but the smallest is just a few kilometres across.

Distant planets

Planets orbit around stars other than the Sun. They are so dim that they are very difficult to see directly in the glare of the stars they orbit. We know of more than 350 distant planets and expect many more to exist.

Young stars

The first stage of a star's life is as a newly formed ball of gas called a protostar. When the gas in its core is hot enough, nuclear reactions start, and the star produces energy and shines.

Life

Planet Earth is the only place in the Universe where life has been found. Life comes in millions of forms, from tiny micro-organisms, such as bacteria, to large mammals, such as humans.

The stars

Earth receives heat and light from the Sun. This hot, spinning ball of luminous gas is one of billions and billions of stars in the Universe. Each follows a life cycle – forming within a gas and dust cloud, changing over time, and eventually dying.

DO NOT FEED THE PLANETS

HUMAN HOUSE

Universal laws

Scientific rules on Earth apply throughout the Universe. For example, gravity keeps our feet on the ground and stops a star's gas drifting off. Chemical elements change state depending on temperature. Water exists elsewhere, but on Earth the temperature is right for it to be liquid.

Super structures

Superclusters link together in a network of long chains and sheets. These are the largest structures of all, existing throughout the Universe. Voids of virtually empty Space separate them.

Galaxies

There are billions of galaxies all around us in the Universe. Each consists of a vast number of stars, together with gas and dust. The Sun is one star among the billions that make up the Milky Way Galaxy.

Galaxy types

Astronomers classify these huge star systems by their shape. The Milky Way is a spiral galaxy – a disc shape with spiral arms. The Sun lies about two-thirds of the distance from the centre to the edge, in one of the spiral arms.

Galaxy clusters

Clusters consist of tens to thousands of galaxies strung together in superclusters. The Milky Way is part of the Local Group cluster. With other galaxy clusters it makes up the Local Supercluster.

Nebulae

Large clouds of mainly hydrogen gas that produce new stars are called nebulae. These include materials cast off by dying stars and that have no definite shape, such as the Horsehead Nebula.

Star clusters

Stars are born in clusters inside dark clouds of gas and dust. At first, clusters remain intact, but over hundreds of millions of years, the stars tend to drift apart.

Maturing stars

Most stars shine steadily just as the Sun is doing now. The Sun is a single star, but many are in partnerships – two stars orbiting around each other.

Stellar ends

Towards the ends of their lives, most stars swell up to become red giant or supergiant stars. Most die slowly, but the more massive ones blow themselves apart suddenly in huge explosions.

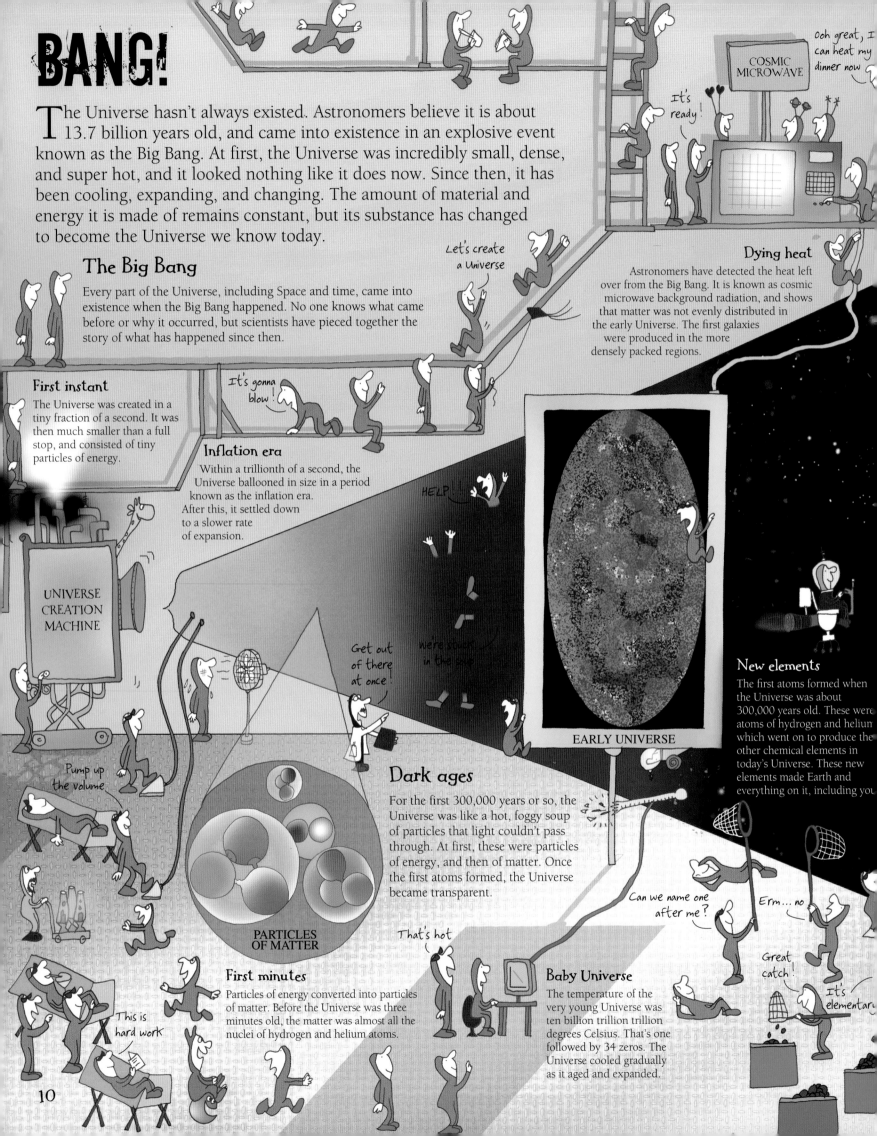

BANG!

The Universe hasn't always existed. Astronomers believe it is about 13.7 billion years old, and came into existence in an explosive event known as the Big Bang. At first, the Universe was incredibly small, dense, and super hot, and it looked nothing like it does now. Since then, it has been cooling, expanding, and changing. The amount of material and energy it is made of remains constant, but its substance has changed to become the Universe we know today.

The Big Bang

Every part of the Universe, including Space and time, came into existence when the Big Bang happened. No one knows what came before or why it occurred, but scientists have pieced together the story of what has happened since then.

First instant

The Universe was created in a tiny fraction of a second. It was then much smaller than a full stop, and consisted of tiny particles of energy.

Inflation era

Within a trillionth of a second, the Universe ballooned in size in a period known as the inflation era. After this, it settled down to a slower rate of expansion.

UNIVERSE CREATION MACHINE

PARTICLES OF MATTER

First minutes

Particles of energy converted into particles of matter. Before the Universe was three minutes old, the matter was almost all the nuclei of hydrogen and helium atoms.

Dark ages

For the first 300,000 years or so, the Universe was like a hot, foggy soup of particles that light couldn't pass through. At first, these were particles of energy, and then of matter. Once the first atoms formed, the Universe became transparent.

EARLY UNIVERSE

Baby Universe

The temperature of the very young Universe was ten billion trillion trillion degrees Celsius. That's one followed by 34 zeros. The Universe cooled gradually as it aged and expanded.

Dying heat

Astronomers have detected the heat left over from the Big Bang. It is known as cosmic microwave background radiation, and shows that matter was not evenly distributed in the early Universe. The first galaxies were produced in the more densely packed regions.

New elements

The first atoms formed when the Universe was about 300,000 years old. These were atoms of hydrogen and helium, which went on to produce the other chemical elements in today's Universe. These new elements made Earth and everything on it, including you.

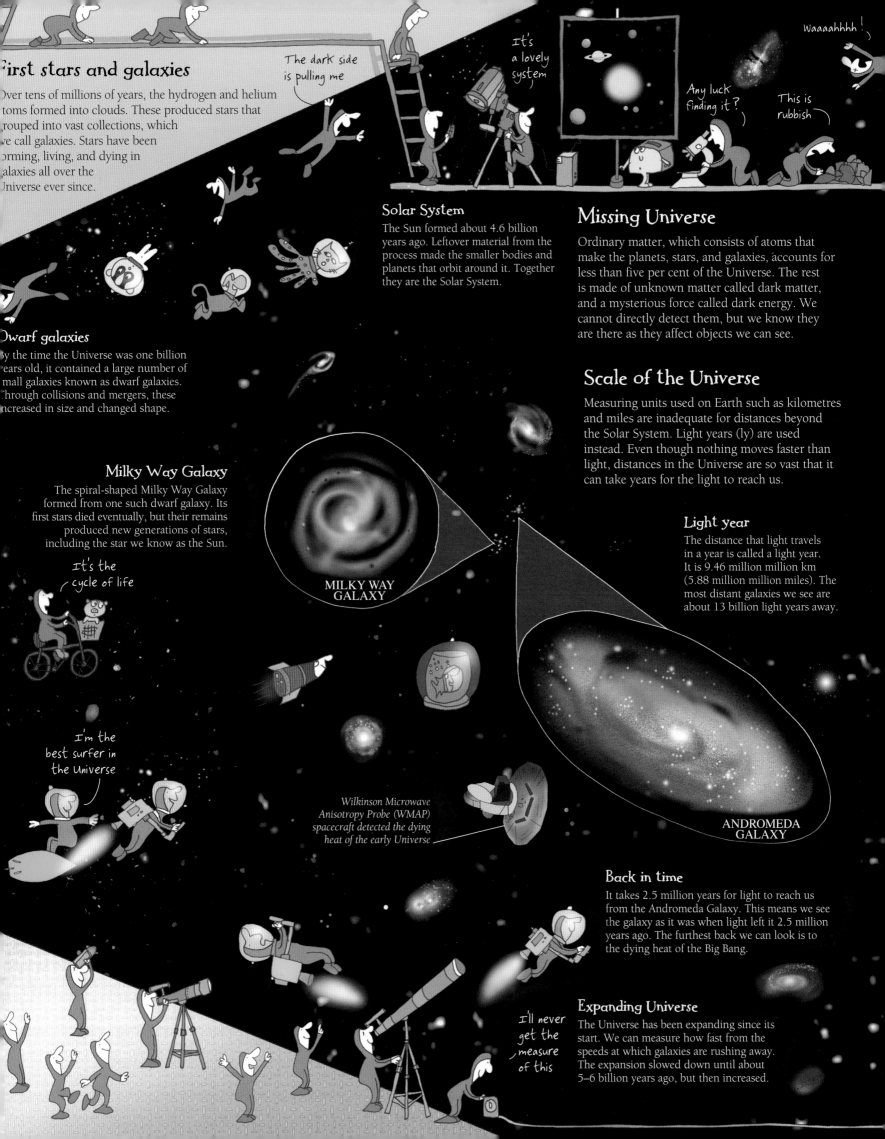

First stars and galaxies

Over tens of millions of years, the hydrogen and helium atoms formed into clouds. These produced stars that grouped into vast collections, which we call galaxies. Stars have been forming, living, and dying in galaxies all over the Universe ever since.

Dwarf galaxies

By the time the Universe was one billion years old, it contained a large number of small galaxies known as dwarf galaxies. Through collisions and mergers, these increased in size and changed shape.

Milky Way Galaxy

The spiral-shaped Milky Way Galaxy formed from one such dwarf galaxy. Its first stars died eventually, but their remains produced new generations of stars, including the star we know as the Sun.

MILKY WAY GALAXY

Wilkinson Microwave Anisotropy Probe (WMAP) spacecraft detected the dying heat of the early Universe

Solar System

The Sun formed about 4.6 billion years ago. Leftover material from the process made the smaller bodies and planets that orbit around it. Together they are the Solar System.

Missing Universe

Ordinary matter, which consists of atoms that make the planets, stars, and galaxies, accounts for less than five per cent of the Universe. The rest is made of unknown matter called dark matter, and a mysterious force called dark energy. We cannot directly detect them, but we know they are there as they affect objects we can see.

Scale of the Universe

Measuring units used on Earth such as kilometres and miles are inadequate for distances beyond the Solar System. Light years (ly) are used instead. Even though nothing moves faster than light, distances in the Universe are so vast that it can take years for the light to reach us.

Light year

The distance that light travels in a year is called a light year. It is 9.46 million million km (5.88 million million miles). The most distant galaxies we see are about 13 billion light years away.

ANDROMEDA GALAXY

Back in time

It takes 2.5 million years for light to reach us from the Andromeda Galaxy. This means we see the galaxy as it was when light left it 2.5 million years ago. The furthest back we can look is to the dying heat of the Big Bang.

Expanding Universe

The Universe has been expanding since its start. We can measure how fast from the speeds at which galaxies are rushing away. The expansion slowed down until about 5–6 billion years ago, but then increased.

Elliptical

These ball-shaped galaxies include those that are round like a football, oval like a rugby ball, and others with shapes in between. Dwarf ellipticals are the most common type of galaxy.

Irregular

Galaxies with no regular shape or form are classed as irregular. These relatively small galaxies are usually rich in gas and dust, with a high proportion of new and young stars.

Dazzling display

Barred spiral

Like spirals, the barred spirals are disc-shaped, but their arms wind out from the ends of a central bar-shaped region of stars. Stars in both types of spiral typically take a few hundred million years for one orbit.

Dark dust lane
cuts across this
active galaxy.

CENTAURUS A

Jet of material

Spiral

Disc-shaped galaxies with curving arms are classed as spirals. A central bulge consists of mainly older stars, and arms rich in bright young stars spiral out from it. Stars exist between the arms, but they are outshone by the brilliance of those in the arms.

Active galaxies

Some galaxies, such as Centaurus A, give off more light than is expected from their stars alone. It comes from material that circles around the supermassive black hole at the galaxy's centre before falling in. Bits of the material are fired out as jets from either side of the hole.

Galaxy shapes

All galaxies are one of four main shapes. These are spiral, barred spiral, elliptical, and irregular. The galaxies don't behave as solid objects; individual stars follow their own orbits around a galaxy's centre.

Blast-off!

Ooooooh!

Udderly brilliant

Arrrr!

What a
whizze

GLITTERING GALAXIES

The Universe is thought to be home to at least 125 billion galaxies. Each consists of a huge number of stars, along with vast amounts of gas and dust, all held together by gravity. They come in a range of shapes and sizes, and differ in the number of stars they contain – from a few million to more than a trillion. Most, if not all, galaxies have a supermassive black hole at their centre.

Names and numbers

Galaxies are identified by catalogue numbers, which are combinations of letters and figures, and by their positions in the sky. Some galaxies also have names that describe what they look like, or are taken from the constellation they are in.

TADPOLE GALAXY

FRIED EGG GALAXY

Tadpole Galaxy

A long streamer of stars and gas extends from a spiral galaxy to form the shape of a tadpole. This odd form is the result of an encounter with another galaxy.

Fried Egg Galaxy

The yellow glow coming from this galaxy's centre resembles a fried egg. It is an active galaxy about a third of the width of the Milky Way Galaxy.

Just give them time...

Two spiral galaxies made of gas, dust, and stars have formed.

400 million years pass and the galaxies are closer together.

Another 250 million years pass and the galaxies merge to form an irregular galaxy.

It's all coming together!

Galaxy clusters

Instead of existing in isolation, galaxies are grouped in clusters. An individual cluster can contain up to a few thousand galaxies. Whatever the number, all clusters occupy a similar-sized spherical region of Space.

Galaxy formation

Billions of years ago, galaxies formed from the merging of groups of stars. These galaxies then interacted, and through collisions and mergers, their shapes, mass, and size changed.

Milky Way

The Sun and the night-time stars all belong to one galaxy, the Milky Way. It is a barred spiral containing about 500 billion stars and measuring 100,000 light years (ly) across, by 4,000 ly deep. Our Sun lies in one of the spiral arms about two-thirds of the distance from the centre to the edge. At the heart of the Milky Way is a supermassive black hole, called Sagittarius A*.

Nope

Remember me?

THE MILKY WAY DAIRY

Path of light

From our position inside the galaxy we see the Milky Way as a band of light across the night sky. The band is also known as the Milky Way.

Our cluster

The Milky Way belongs to a cluster of more than 40 galaxies known as the Local Group. Most are dwarf galaxies, orbiting the two biggest – the Milky Way and Andromeda galaxies.

We'll be here 'til the cows come home

About now then

Ready for the milk round?

Your churn!

...me for ...d Daisy

COSMIC CAREERS FAIR

Arthur Eddington

In the 1920s, British astronomer Arthur Eddington showed that a star's energy comes from nuclear reactions within.

Cecilia Payne–Gaposchkin

In the 1920s, this British star-gazer found that stars are made mainly of hydrogen.

Fred Hoyle

British cosmologist Hoyle showed how elements are made in stars and coined the phrase "Big Bang".

Fred Whipple

American astronomer Fred Whipple discovered six comets. In the 1950s, he explained that a comet is a dirty snowball.

Subrahmanyan Chandrasekhar

Born in India, Chandrasekhar is known for his work on stellar structure and the evolution of stars.

Vera Rubin

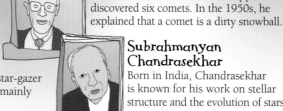

Wow!

Astronomers grew certain that dark matter exists after US astronomer Rubin showed its gravity affects how stars move inside galaxies.

Edwin Hubble

In the 1920s, the USA's Edwin Hubble discovered that the Universe is full of galaxies, and that it is expanding.

Computers

Astronomers use computers in a variety of ways, such as to control telescopes and spacecraft, to record, store, and analyse data, and to make detailed calculations that would otherwise take months. Computers are also used to simulate scenarios in Space, such as two galaxies colliding.

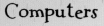

We're on a collision course

Hello, Fred

Spacecraft

Astronomers stay on Earth but send robotic craft to explore the Solar System at close range. On arrival at their destination, telescopes and other instruments on board the craft collect and record data. This is then relayed to the astronomers back on Earth.

What news?

Don't keep us in suspense!

oooh! There's a message coming through

Domes stand several storeys high at Mauna Kea, Hawaii, home to some of Earth's largest telescopes

Observatories

Telescopes are housed in dome- or drum-shaped buildings. One or a group of these is called an observatory. The world's best observatories are located on the top of mountains, well away from city lights and where the air is thin, clear, and still.

A breath of fresh air

It's just an observation

Astronomer's life

Scientists who study the objects in the Universe are called astronomers. They study from Earth, relying on information travelling through Space. Objects are observed and data is collected, and an astronomer uses scientific and mathematical knowledge to find out more. A single astronomer doesn't study everything in the Universe but specializes in one aspect. Most work for a government organization, based at a laboratory, university, or observatory.

Astrophysicists

Many astronomers are astrophysicists concerned with the physical properties of objects. Astrophysicists can be grouped together as those interested in stars, galaxies, or Solar System objects.

Cosmologists

Astronomers studying the Universe as a whole are known as cosmologists. They are interested in how the Universe started, how it developed, and what it will be like in the future.

You got Space Invaders?

I'm monitoring the situation

Find out more

One of the best ways to get involved in astronomy is to join a local club. Members share their knowledge, visiting astronomers give classes and tips, and you'll have the chance to use a telescope.

ASTRO CLUB

Members only

But I'm a big star

Looking up

You can start to become an astronomer by looking up at the sky on a night when there are no clouds or Moon. With the naked eye, you can see about 300 stars from the city, about 1,000 from a village, and about 3,000 from the countryside where it is darkest.

Amateur astronomers

Not everyone involved in astronomy does it for a living. Lots of people enjoy astronomy as a hobby and get pleasure from seeing the objects in the Universe at first hand. Some are regular observers who make discoveries that support the professional astronomers in their work.

You're such an amateur!

Final analysis

Astronomers spend little time observing the sky because telescopes are so efficient at collecting data. Instead, most of their time is spent studying the data. Regardless of how good the data is, however, it is the astronomer's analysis and interpretation that produces successful results.

Analyse this

Sharing knowledge

Astronomers publish their work for others to see, and also meet to discuss and share ideas. They build on the latest knowledge, deciding on new questions to ask about the Universe and how to go about answering them. Through the astronomers' work we can all understand and enjoy the Universe.

I want to be a gastronomer

This is astronomical stuff

Instruments

An instrument called a spectrograph can be attached to a telescope. This splits light into its spectrum – the rainbow band of colours. Astronomers use this to work out the types of gas in a star and the star's temperature.

Whoa!

Telescopes

Astronomers have a number of tools to help them study the Universe. Most important is the telescope, which collects light and other types of energy from objects in Space. Huge specialist instruments are attached to telescopes to help astronomers process and analyse the data.

Not a great view

It's instrumental to our work

Planetary geologists

The surface and internal structure of the rocky planets and their moons are studied by planetary geologists. They also study the origin and history of these worlds.

Rock but no roll

Rock on

Telescope operators

One of the astronomer's key supporters is a telescope operator. This person looks after the world's best telescopes, collecting data for astronomers to use.

Radio astronomers

Some astronomers concentrate on the non-visual wavelengths coming from Space objects. These include the radio astronomer who is an expert on radio signals.

Give us a wave!

Turn on, tune in...

Space astronomers

Robotic craft work in Space on behalf of astronomers. A Space astronomer decides on the instruments for the craft, designs them, and analyses the data when it comes in.

I'm Spaced out

15

EYE ON THE UNIVERSE

Astronomers use telescopes to look deep into the Universe. Like giant eyes, they collect light from objects and use it to produce images. Yet, telescopes are much better than eyes. They collect a lot more light, and produce magnified images. In addition to optical telescopes, which collect light, others collect different forms of energy. These reveal new aspects of familiar objects, and identify things that would otherwise remain undiscovered.

Telescope

A telescope has a main mirror (sometimes a lens) to collect light and focus it. A smaller mirror usually intercepts the focused beam of light and sends it into an instrument, a camera, or someone's eye.

Eye eye

Eyes on the prize

Eye see!

Second mirror focuses light from main mirror onto third mirror

Light passes through telescope's open structure to main mirror

Main mirror

The bigger the main mirror, the more light it collects, enabling astronomers to see fainter and more distant objects. Large mirrors sag under their own weight, so small ones work together as one big mirror.

Main mirror made of 36 small mirrors is 10 m (33 ft) across

Third mirror sends light to instrument box

Mount

A telescope is supported on a mount, which allows it to move. Once on its target object automatic controls keep it fixed on the object as Earth turns.

Mount

The view

A camera or spectrograph is positioned where the image would form. The light is recorded on an electronic chip and viewed on a computer.

Instrument box houses camera or spectrograph

TORCHES

Stay focused

Let me sh some light

Space energy

Light and other energy forms travel in waves of differing length. By collecting a range of these with special telescopes, we get a more complete view of the Universe. Not all the wavelengths reach Earth's surface. Shorter ones, such as X-rays, cannot penetrate Earth's atmosphere.

Gamma rays have the shortest wavelengths, and are emitted by supernovae

X-rays are released by stellar material falling into a black hole

Ultraviolet (UV) rays are given off very strongly by stars hotter than the Sun

Light rays come from stars, and sunlight is reflected by objects such as planets

Infrared rays are collected from cooler objects such as star-forming nebulae

Microwaves are short radio waves and are produced by the dying heat of the Big Bang

Radio waves are the longest, and have been used to discover otherwise invisible galaxies

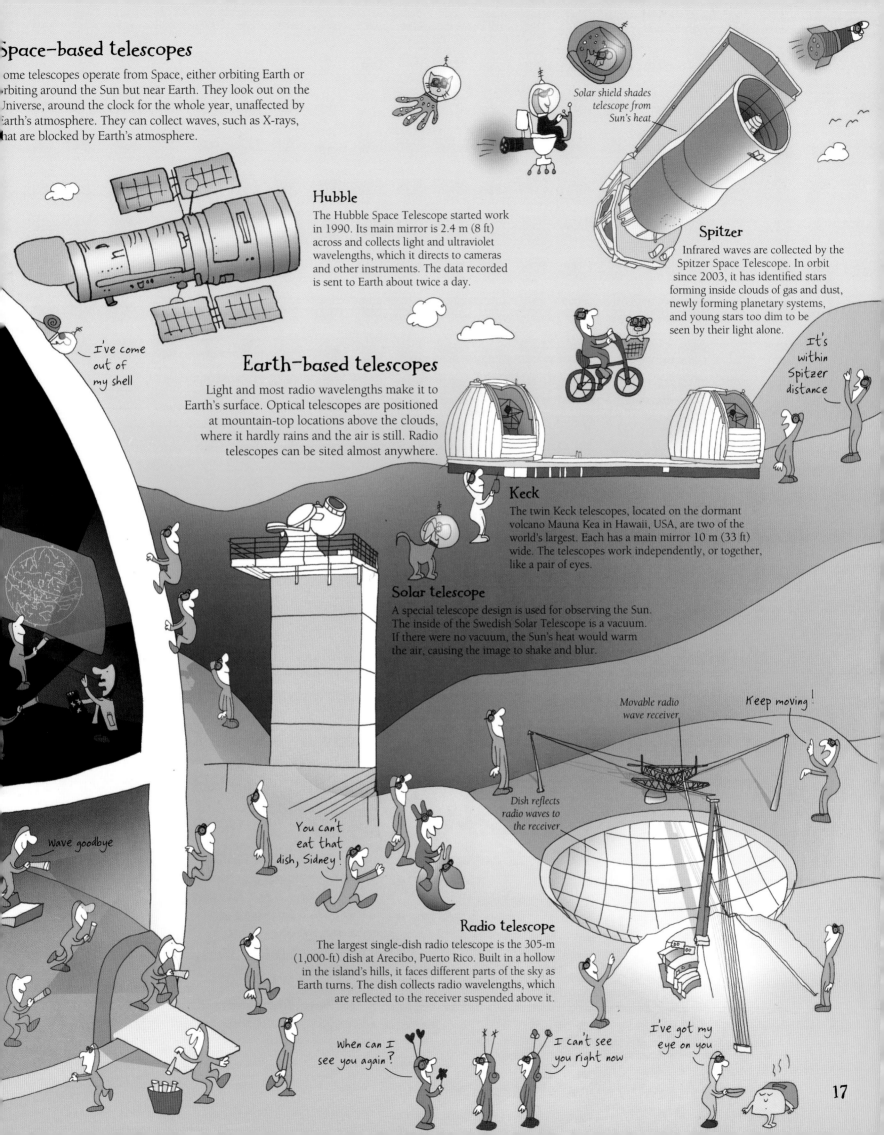

Space-based telescopes

Some telescopes operate from Space, either orbiting Earth or orbiting around the Sun but near Earth. They look out on the Universe, around the clock for the whole year, unaffected by Earth's atmosphere. They can collect waves, such as X-rays, that are blocked by Earth's atmosphere.

Solar shield shades telescope from Sun's heat

Hubble

The Hubble Space Telescope started work in 1990. Its main mirror is 2.4 m (8 ft) across and collects light and ultraviolet wavelengths, which it directs to cameras and other instruments. The data recorded is sent to Earth about twice a day.

Spitzer

Infrared waves are collected by the Spitzer Space Telescope. In orbit since 2003, it has identified stars forming inside clouds of gas and dust, newly forming planetary systems, and young stars too dim to be seen by their light alone.

I've come out of my shell

It's within Spitzer distance

Earth-based telescopes

Light and most radio wavelengths make it to Earth's surface. Optical telescopes are positioned at mountain-top locations above the clouds, where it hardly rains and the air is still. Radio telescopes can be sited almost anywhere.

Keck

The twin Keck telescopes, located on the dormant volcano Mauna Kea in Hawaii, USA, are two of the world's largest. Each has a main mirror 10 m (33 ft) wide. The telescopes work independently, or together, like a pair of eyes.

Solar telescope

A special telescope design is used for observing the Sun. The inside of the Swedish Solar Telescope is a vacuum. If there were no vacuum, the Sun's heat would warm the air, causing the image to shake and blur.

Movable radio wave receiver

Keep moving!

Dish reflects radio waves to the receiver

wave goodbye

You can't eat that dish, Sidney!

Radio telescope

The largest single-dish radio telescope is the 305-m (1,000-ft) dish at Arecibo, Puerto Rico. Built in a hollow in the island's hills, it faces different parts of the sky as Earth turns. The dish collects radio wavelengths, which are reflected to the receiver suspended above it.

When can I see you again?

I can't see you right now

I've got my eye on you

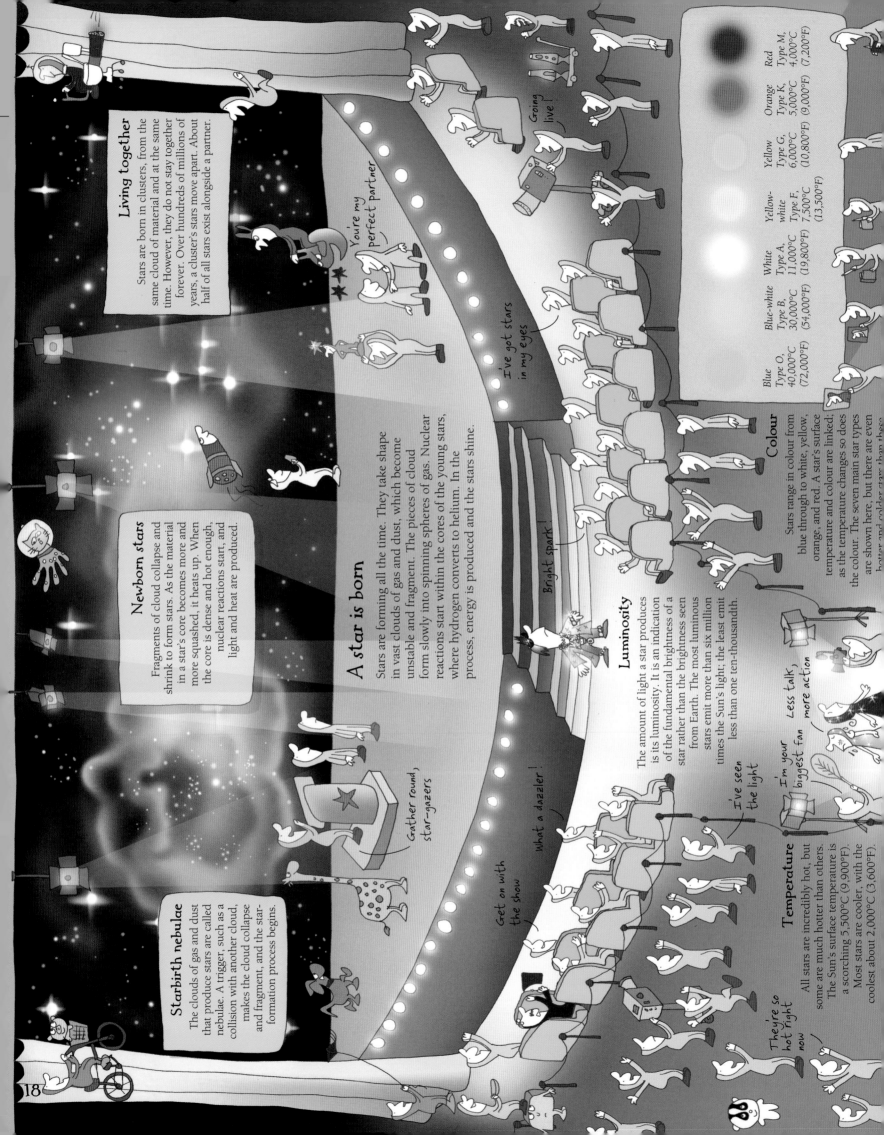

Living together

Stars are born in clusters, from the same cloud of material and at the same time. However, they do not stay together forever. Over hundreds of millions of years, a cluster's stars move apart. About half of all stars exist alongside a partner.

Newborn stars

Fragments of cloud collapse and shrink to form stars. As the material in a star's core becomes more and more squashed, it heats up. When the core is dense and hot enough, nuclear reactions start, and light and heat are produced.

Starbirth nebulae

The clouds of gas and dust that produce stars are called nebulae. A trigger, such as a collision with another cloud, makes the cloud collapse and fragment, and the star-formation process begins.

A star is born

Stars are forming all the time. They take shape in vast clouds of gas and dust, which become unstable and fragment. The pieces of cloud form slowly into spinning spheres of gas. Nuclear reactions start within the cores of the young stars, where hydrogen converts to helium. In the process, energy is produced and the stars shine.

Luminosity

The amount of light a star produces is its luminosity. It is an indication of the fundamental brightness of a star rather than the brightness seen from Earth. The most luminous stars emit more than six million times the Sun's light; the least emit less than one ten-thousandth.

Temperature

All stars are incredibly hot, but some are much hotter than others. The Sun's surface temperature is a scorching 5,500°C (9,900°F). Most stars are cooler, with the coolest about 2,000°C (3,600°F).

Colour

Stars range in colour from blue through to white, yellow, orange, and red. A star's surface temperature and colour are linked; as the temperature changes so does the colour. The seven main star types are shown here, but there are even hotter and colder stars than these.

Blue Type O, 40,000°C (72,000°F)	Blue-white Type B, 30,000°C (54,000°F)	White Type A, 11,000°C (19,800°F)	Yellow-white Type F, 7,500°C (13,500°F)	Yellow Type G, 6,000°C (10,800°F)	Orange Type K, 5,000°C (9,000°F)	Red Type M, 4,000°C (7,200°F)

Going live!

You're my perfect partner

I've got stars in my eyes

Bright spark!

Gather round, star-gazers

Get on with the show

What a dazzler!

I've seen the light

I'm your biggest fan

Less talk, more action

They're so hot right now

STARS OF THE SHOW

All stars, except the Sun, are so far away that they appear as pinpoints of twinkling light to our eyes. They may look the same, but each star is unique and has its own characteristics. Stars differ in size, temperature, colour, luminosity, and mass. These attributes change as a star ages and moves from one stage of its life to the next. Of chief importance is mass – the amount of material a star is made of – because this determines the length and course of a star's life.

Gravity and pressure

A constant battle between gravity and pressure occurs inside stars. A star's gravity pulls its material into the centre, while the pressure of the central gas pushes the material out. The forces counterbalance each other and maintain the star's spherical shape.

Density

The size of a star is related to the density of its material. Two stars can be made of the same mass, but they can take up different volumes of space. When the material is spread out, the star is large, and when tightly packed, the star is much smaller.

Shape

Stars are spherical whatever their size and mass. They are not star-shaped but appear that way sometimes because of how their light passes through Earth's atmosphere. The light is bent and wobbled by bubbles of hot and cold air, giving the stars a pointed edge.

Mass

The amount of material that makes up the Sun is described as one solar mass. Other stars are measured in multiples or fractions of this. The most massive are about 100 times more massive, while the least are just one tenth of the Sun's mass.

Star material

Stars are huge spinning globes of hot, glowing gas. They are mainly hydrogen and partly helium, together with small amounts of other elements. A star's gravity pulls the gas in and keeps it together. Much of this gas is squashed inside the star's core, where it produces energy, such as heat and light.

Size

The mass of a star hardly changes during its life, but a star's size can vary greatly. The Sun is 1.4 million km (0.8 million miles) across. The largest stars are more than 1,000 times the Sun's width; the smallest are about one hundredth of it.

Radiation in form of light

Force of gravity

Internal pressure

I'm feeling the pressure

Wowsers!

You better shape up

Larger than life

Size matters

I skipped dinner, that's all

This show is running shipshape

Bit of a squeeze

VIPs only

Non-VIPs

Give me some space

Who invited them?

Make way! Big egos coming through

But you loved me in the film

It's called acting

That's about the size of it

Are these teeth real?

Sunspots

Dark patches, called sunspots, appear periodically and last for weeks at a time. They are relatively cool regions of the photosphere produced when the Sun's magnetic field interrupts rising heat.

Sunspots are thousands of kilometres wide

Coronal mass ejections

Colossal bubbles consisting of billions of tonnes of gas are blasted out of the Sun. Known as coronal mass ejections, they move through the atmosphere and into Space.

Spicules

Short-lived jets of gas, called spicules, leap up continually from the photosphere. They are tiny compared to the Sun, each measuring a few thousand kilometres in length.

Prominences

Giant clouds and sheets of relatively cool gas that loop and arch from the surface are called prominences. They extend out into Space for hundreds of thousands of kilometres.

Temperature

The surface temperature is 5,500°C (9,900°F), and this gives the Sun its yellow colour. If the photosphere were cooler, the Sun would be red. If it were hotter, it would be white.

Atmosphere

Beyond the photosphere is the Sun's atmosphere, which is not normally visible. The part immediately above the Sun is the chromosphere. More distant is the corona, which stretches out for millions of kilometres.

Ra

The ancient Egyptians believed their Sun god, Ra, sailed through the underworld each night, reappearing in the east every morning to journey across the daytime sky. He carried the Sun's disc on his falcon head.

Granulation

The photosphere consists of 1,000-km- (620-mile-) wide cells of rising gas that constantly renew themselves. Together they make the Sun's visible surface resemble orange peel.

Visible features

The Sun is not solid but has a visible surface. This is known as the photosphere. Its appearance changes constantly. Hot gas rises and then falls as it cools. Sometimes there are violent releases of energy, flinging material far out into Space.

Apollo

Handsome Apollo, the son of Zeus (the supreme god of Greek mythology), was associated with the Sun. Each day he drove his horse-drawn chariot across the sky to give light to the world.

OUR STAR

The Sun is the closest star to Earth. Like other stars, it is a huge ball of glowing gas kept together by gravity. Measuring about 1.4 million km (0.8 million miles) across, it appears as a disc of light in Earth's daytime sky. It is mostly made of hydrogen and helium, and small amounts of about 90 other elements. The Sun has been shining for at least 4.6 billion years and will do so for another five billion.

Warning

Never look directly at the Sun, either with the naked eye or through an instrument. Its bright light will burn your retina (the membrane at the back of the eye) and cause permanent damage.

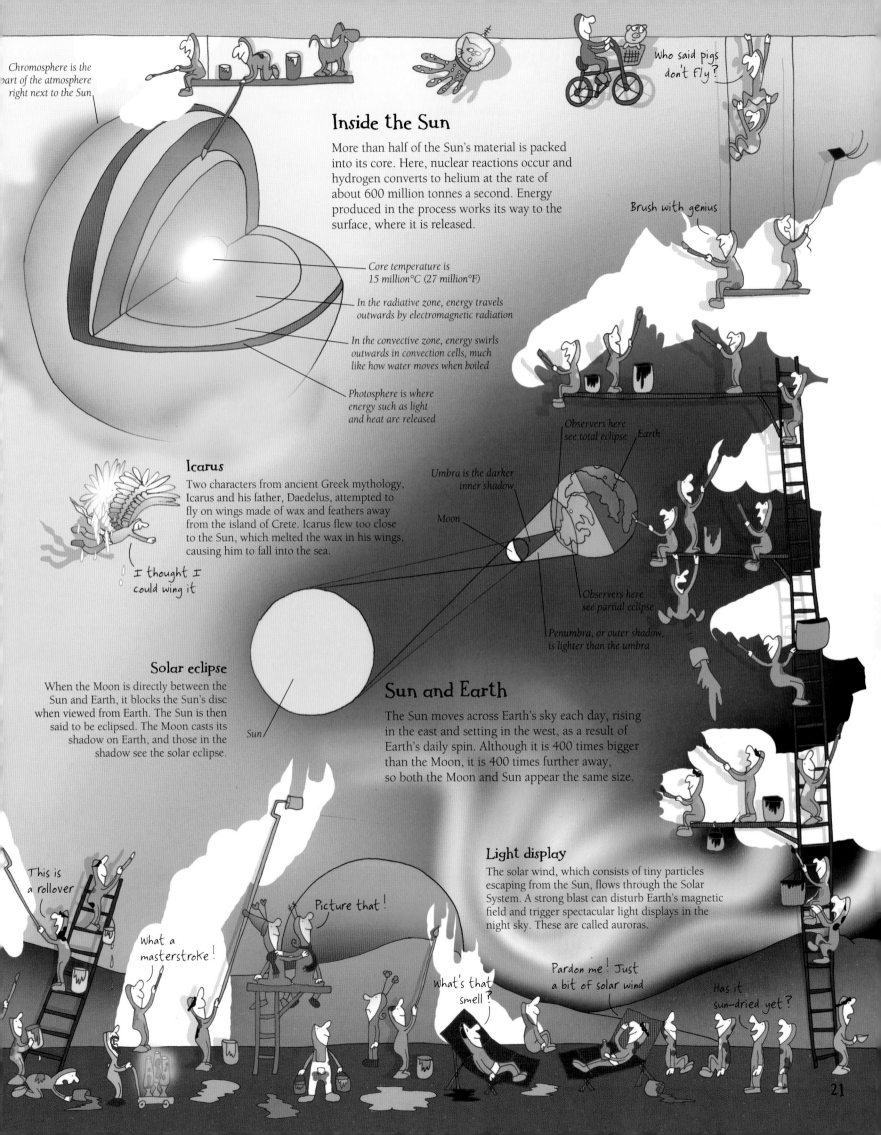

Chromosphere is the part of the atmosphere right next to the Sun

Inside the Sun

More than half of the Sun's material is packed into its core. Here, nuclear reactions occur and hydrogen converts to helium at the rate of about 600 million tonnes a second. Energy produced in the process works its way to the surface, where it is released.

Core temperature is 15 million°C (27 million°F)

In the radiative zone, energy travels outwards by electromagnetic radiation

In the convective zone, energy swirls outwards in convection cells, much like how water moves when boiled

Photosphere is where energy such as light and heat are released

Icarus

Two characters from ancient Greek mythology, Icarus and his father, Daedelus, attempted to fly on wings made of wax and feathers away from the island of Crete. Icarus flew too close to the Sun, which melted the wax in his wings, causing him to fall into the sea.

I thought I could wing it

Solar eclipse

When the Moon is directly between the Sun and Earth, it blocks the Sun's disc when viewed from Earth. The Sun is then said to be eclipsed. The Moon casts its shadow on Earth, and those in the shadow see the solar eclipse.

Sun

Observers here see total eclipse

Earth

Umbra is the darker inner shadow

Moon

Observers here see partial eclipse

Penumbra, or outer shadow, is lighter than the umbra

Sun and Earth

The Sun moves across Earth's sky each day, rising in the east and setting in the west, as a result of Earth's daily spin. Although it is 400 times bigger than the Moon, it is 400 times further away, so both the Moon and Sun appear the same size.

Light display

The solar wind, which consists of tiny particles escaping from the Sun, flows through the Solar System. A strong blast can disturb Earth's magnetic field and trigger spectacular light displays in the night sky. These are called auroras.

Who said pigs don't fly?

Brush with genius

This is a rollover

What a masterstroke!

Picture that!

what's that smell?

Pardon me! Just a bit of solar wind

Has it sun-dried yet?

STARRY, STARRY NIGHT

Thousands of individual stars shine out in the night sky. Each is a huge luminous globe but so far away that even the nearest appears as a pinpoint of light. The brightest can be linked by imaginary lines to create star patterns, which stargazers have used for about 4,000 years. These patterns help us find our way among the stars, and we can use them to trace the path of the Sun, Moon, and planets across the sky.

Star patterns

The patterns take the form of a person, creature, or object. Just over half are characters from Ancient Greek mythology, such as Orion the great hunter, and his two hunting dogs, Canis Minor and Canis Major.

Starry Path

All the stars seen in Earth's night sky belong to the spiral-shaped Milky Way Galaxy. The star-packed path of milky light that spans the night sky is our view into the galaxy's disc. The brightest and broadest part of the path is the view into the galaxy's centre.

Zodiac

The 12 constellations of the zodiac form the backdrop to the path of the Sun, Moon, and planets through the stars. The name comes from the Greek for "animal." Apart from Libra, the zodiac constellations circling the sky represent living creatures.

Constellations

The sky surrounding Earth is divided into 88 straight-edged pieces, which interlock like the parts of a jigsaw. Each one is a constellation made up of a star pattern and the sky immediately around it.

Optical illusion

The stars in a constellation have no real link with each other. They only appear to be connected, and are really at great distances from Earth and from each other. Seen from another direction they would make a different pattern.

Changing views

The constellations seen depend on a stargazer's location on Earth, and the date and time. The view differs from north or south. At a fixed location it alters gradually from night to night as Earth travels around the Sun, and in the evening as Earth makes its daily spin.

Eeek! That bull's charging!

Pleiades

Taurus (bull)

Aldebaran

Constellation boundary

Orion (hunter)

Betelgeuse

Gemini (twins)

Monoceros (unicorn)

Canis Minor (small dog)

Canis Major (big dog)

Sirius

Milky Way path

Lepus (hare)

Eridanus (river)

Columba (dove)

The dove from above

Puppis (ship's stern)

What's your starsign?

My lucky stars

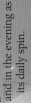
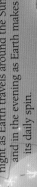

Name game

Most constellations have two names: their Latin name and their common name. For instance, Taurus is commonly known as the bull. The brightest stars are known by a letter of the Greek alphabet – alpha, beta, and so on – along with the constellation name. Some have two names – Alpha Tauri is also called Aldebaran.

Lyra (lyre)

Tucana (toucan)

Corona Borealis (northern crown)

Mensa (mountain)

Cygnus (swan)

Coma Berenices (Berenice's hair)

Camelopardalis (giraffe)

Delphinus (dolphin)

Monoceros (unicorn)

Star brightness

The stars in the sky differ in brilliance. One of the first stargazers, Hipparchus, noticed this and classed them according to brightness. The scale we use today – called the apparent magnitude scale – is based on his system. The brightest star in Earth's sky is Sirius in Canis Major.

Yes, it's really in a class of its own

It's so bright!

I'm starry-eyed

Have a nice trip!

I've fallen for you

Your feet smell

Now's not the time for complaints

Get a grip!

Wandering stars

As Earth spins, the stars move across the sky, fixed in their relative positions. Some bright dots seen in the zodiac constellations appear to move slowly among the stars. These are the planets. The word "planet" comes from the Greek for "wanderer". Unlike the stars, planets have no light of their own but shine by reflected sunlight.

Speak up, Sidney

Once upon a time...

WANDERING STARS

Fuzzy stars

Some of the starry lights in the sky are not pinpoints but appear fuzzy. They could be a comet passing through Earth's sky as it loops around the Sun, a nebula of gas and dust giving birth to new stars, or a distant galaxy. Their real form is apparent only when seen through a powerful telescope.

Shooting stars

Trails of light that appear periodically in the night sky are popularly known as "shooting stars", but are actually meteors. Lasting less than a second, they are produced by fragments of comet speeding through Earth's atmosphere.

I'm starstruck

I've got neckache

I was born under a wandering star

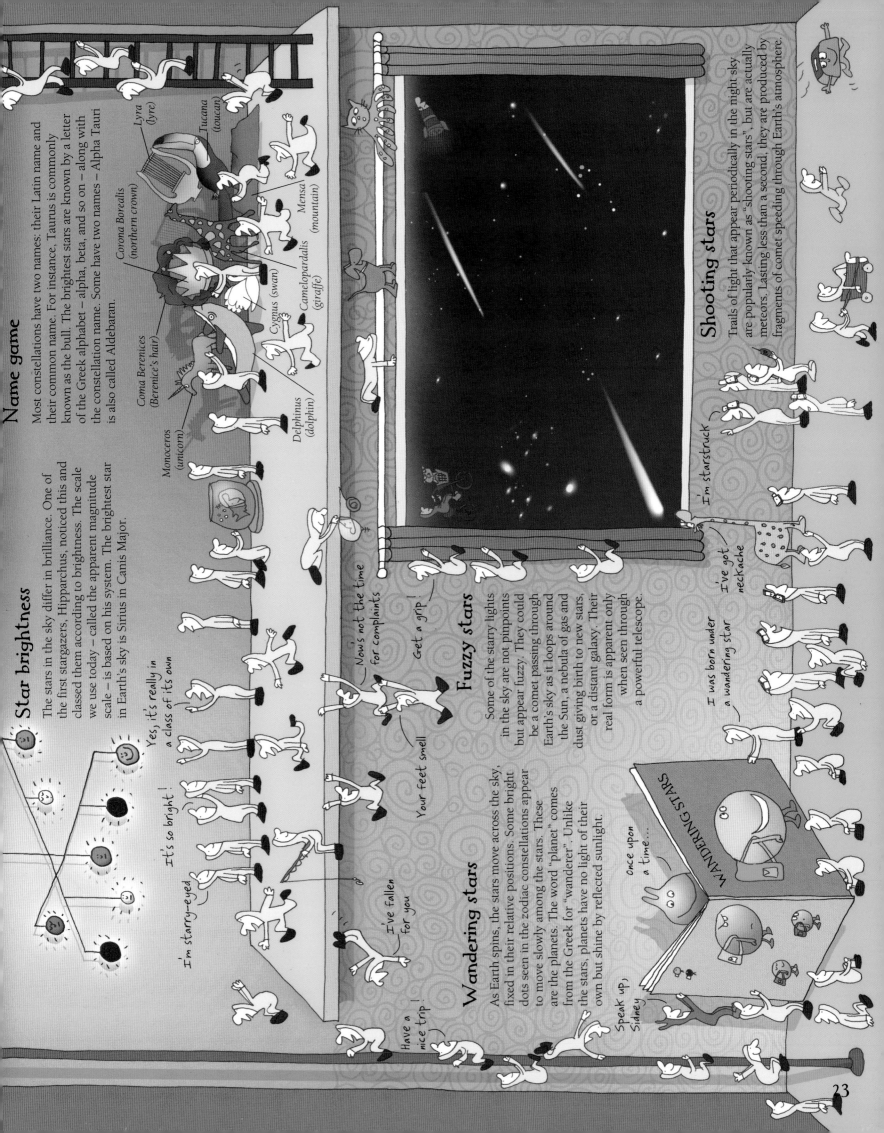

RECYCLED UNIVERSE

Stars do not live forever, but they do have very long lives. Sun-like stars shine brightly for billions of years, while more massive ones last just a few million years. The mass of a star – the amount of material it is made of – not only determines the length of its life, but also how it dies. Most stars fade away, but the most massive end their lives abruptly. As stars die they shed material, which helps create a new generation of stars.

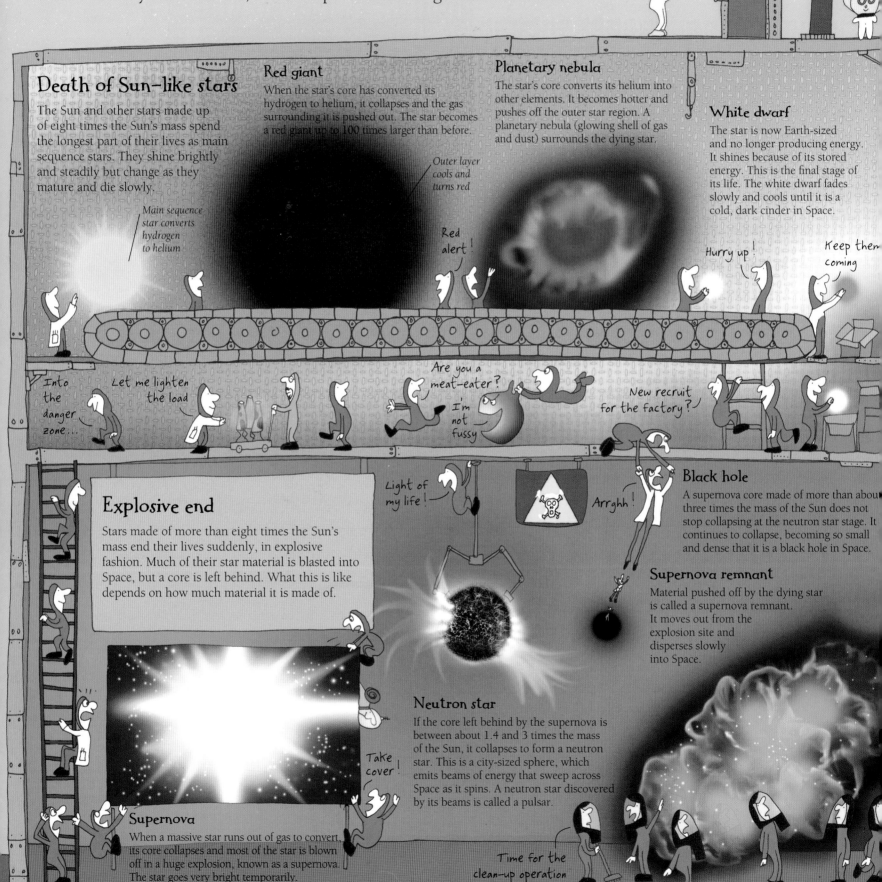

Death of Sun-like stars

The Sun and other stars made up of eight times the Sun's mass spend the longest part of their lives as main sequence stars. They shine brightly and steadily but change as they mature and die slowly.

Main sequence star converts hydrogen to helium

Red giant

When the star's core has converted its hydrogen to helium, it collapses and the gas surrounding it is pushed out. The star becomes a red giant up to 100 times larger than before.

Outer layer cools and turns red

Planetary nebula

The star's core converts its helium into other elements. It becomes hotter and pushes off the outer star region. A planetary nebula (glowing shell of gas and dust) surrounds the dying star.

White dwarf

The star is now Earth-sized and no longer producing energy. It shines because of its stored energy. This is the final stage of its life. The white dwarf fades slowly and cools until it is a cold, dark cinder in Space.

Explosive end

Stars made of more than eight times the Sun's mass end their lives suddenly, in explosive fashion. Much of their star material is blasted into Space, but a core is left behind. What this is like depends on how much material it is made of.

Black hole

A supernova core made of more than about three times the mass of the Sun does not stop collapsing at the neutron star stage. It continues to collapse, becoming so small and dense that it is a black hole in Space.

Supernova remnant

Material pushed off by the dying star is called a supernova remnant. It moves out from the explosion site and disperses slowly into Space.

Neutron star

If the core left behind by the supernova is between about 1.4 and 3 times the mass of the Sun, it collapses to form a neutron star. This is a city-sized sphere, which emits beams of energy that sweep across Space as it spins. A neutron star discovered by its beams is called a pulsar.

Supernova

When a massive star runs out of gas to convert, its core collapses and most of the star is blown off in a huge explosion, known as a supernova. The star goes very bright temporarily.

I am star stuff!

The Sun is mainly hydrogen and helium, but also includes small amounts of other elements. Earth formed close to the Sun from the same cloud of matter. Humans are material made from Earth's elements, so everything in our bodies was once in a star.

Star generations

Nuclear reactions inside the first stars produced new elements, which were dispersed when the stars died. This enriched material formed a new generation of stars, creating further amounts of new elements.

First stars

When the Universe was young, the only chemical elements it contained were hydrogen and helium, so the first stars were formed from these two elements.

HYDROGEN

HELIUM

It's elementary

Most of the chemical elements in the Universe today, such as oxygen and carbon, were made by stars. Many were created by nuclear reactions inside stars, but others came from supernova explosions. The variety of elements Earth is made of came from stars.

Stage 3

Dense clumps form in the clouds and collapse to form stars. The brilliant light of young stars clears parts of the clouds away and makes them glow.

Stage 2

In the mixed up material, clouds are drawn together by gravity. These clouds are huge, cold, and dark.

Stage 4

The stars are now in the prime of their lives. They shine steadily as nuclear reactions deep within them convert their hydrogen into helium and other elements.

Stage 1

Gas and dust is shed by stars nearing the ends of their lives. Over millions of years, it spreads out and mixes with thin hydrogen gas between the stars.

Stellar recycling

Material from dying stars, such as that pushed off when a supernova explodes, collects together as a vast cloud that will produce new stars. Successive generations of stars have been created in this way throughout the history of the Universe.

Meet the family

Earth is part of a Space family called the Solar System, formed from a vast cloud of gas and dust about 4.6 billion years ago. It consists of the Sun and a number of objects orbiting around it. After the Sun, the most prominent family members are eight planets, but there are more smaller bodies. The planets were once thought to be unique, but we now know that other stars have planets orbiting around them, too.

Solar System

The four closest planets to the Sun are the rock and metal worlds of Mercury, Venus, Earth, and Mars. Beyond these are four planets known as the giants: Jupiter, Saturn, Uranus, and Neptune. Each planet and object in the system follows a path around the Sun, and one complete circuit of the Sun is called an orbit. As each object orbits, it also spins.

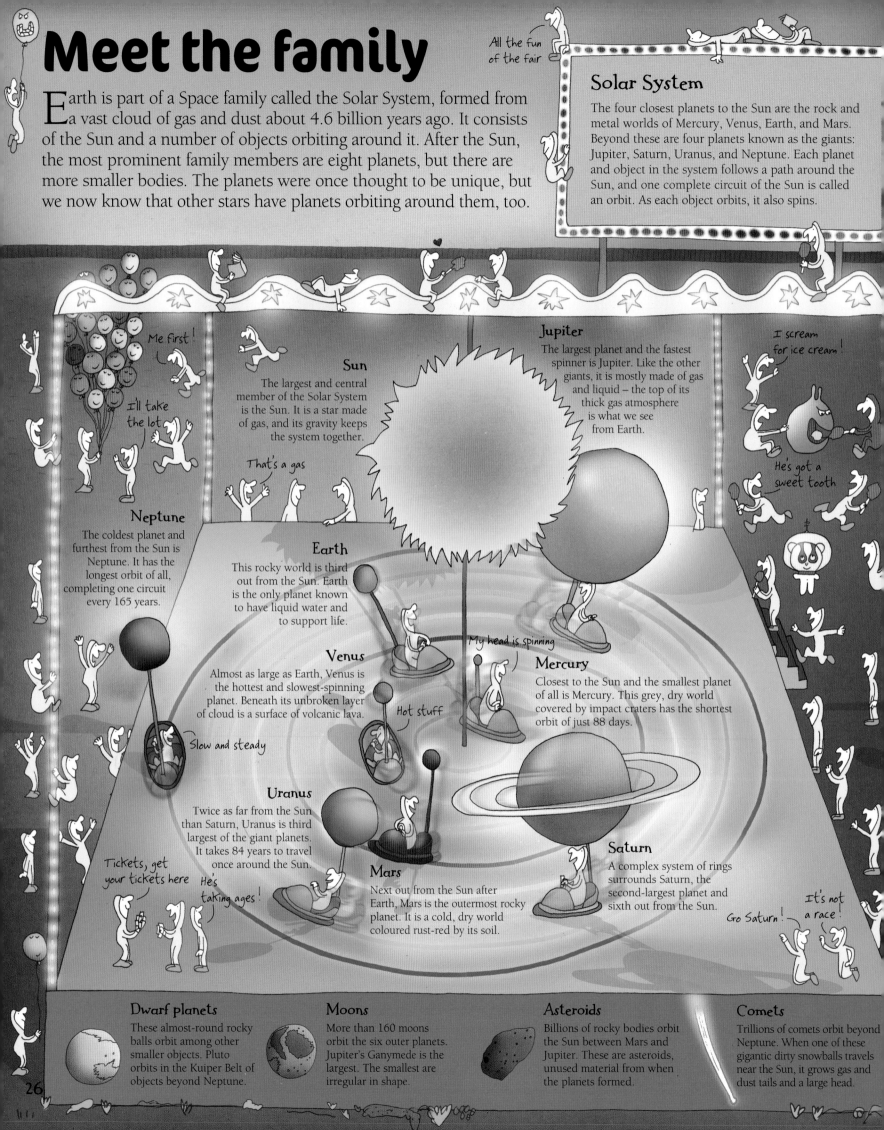

All the fun of the fair

Me first!

I'll take the lot

That's a gas

I scream for ice cream!

He's got a sweet tooth

Jupiter

The largest planet and the fastest spinner is Jupiter. Like the other giants, it is mostly made of gas and liquid – the top of its thick gas atmosphere is what we see from Earth.

Sun

The largest and central member of the Solar System is the Sun. It is a star made of gas, and its gravity keeps the system together.

Neptune

The coldest planet and furthest from the Sun is Neptune. It has the longest orbit of all, completing one circuit every 165 years.

Earth

This rocky world is third out from the Sun. Earth is the only planet known to have liquid water and to support life.

My head is spinning

Venus

Almost as large as Earth, Venus is the hottest and slowest-spinning planet. Beneath its unbroken layer of cloud is a surface of volcanic lava.

Hot stuff

Mercury

Closest to the Sun and the smallest planet of all is Mercury. This grey, dry world covered by impact craters has the shortest orbit of just 88 days.

Slow and steady

Uranus

Twice as far from the Sun than Saturn, Uranus is third largest of the giant planets. It takes 84 years to travel once around the Sun.

Tickets, get your tickets here

He's taking ages!

Mars

Next out from the Sun after Earth, Mars is the outermost rocky planet. It is a cold, dry world coloured rust-red by its soil.

Saturn

A complex system of rings surrounds Saturn, the second-largest planet and sixth out from the Sun.

Go Saturn!

It's not a race!

Dwarf planets

These almost-round rocky balls orbit among other smaller objects. Pluto orbits in the Kuiper Belt of objects beyond Neptune.

Moons

More than 160 moons orbit the six outer planets. Jupiter's Ganymede is the largest. The smallest are irregular in shape.

Asteroids

Billions of rocky bodies orbit the Sun between Mars and Jupiter. These are asteroids, unused material from when the planets formed.

Comets

Trillions of comets orbit beyond Neptune. When one of these gigantic dirty snowballs travels near the Sun, it grows gas and dust tails and a large head.

Birth of the Solar System

The Solar System formed from a cloud of gas and dust known as the solar nebula. As the cloud spun, gravity pulled material into the centre. This formed the Sun. Left-over material settled into a disc around the Sun. Over millions of years, pieces of this material bumped and joined together and made larger and larger pieces, eventually forming the planets.

1. Solar nebula

Gas and dust collected together to make a huge cloud, which spun and contracted. Material squashed in the centre became hot, and formed the Sun.

2. Coming together

Close to the Sun, rocky and metallic material formed the rocky planets. In the outer colder regions, rock, metal, snow, and ice formed the cores of the giants, which attracted huge amounts of gas.

Sun takes shape in the centre

Rotating and flattening disc of material

It's taking shape

Pieces of material join together

3. Planets formed

Leftover chunks of material were drawn into the Sun and destroyed, or pushed out of the Solar System. Others formed the asteroids, Kuiper Belt Objects, and comets.

Neptune

Venus

Saturn

Earth

Mercury

Mars

Asteroids

Uranus

Jupiter

Other planetary systems

Until the 1990s, the Sun was the only known star with planets. Since then, more than 350 planets orbiting other stars have been discovered. Known as exoplanets, they are difficult to detect. Nearly all have been found because they affect the motion or light of their star. Massive Jupiter-like worlds are the easiest to find.

PLANETARY HOOPLA

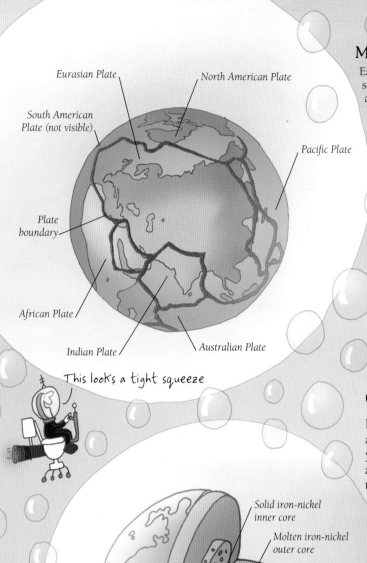

Eurasian Plate

North American Plate

South American Plate (not visible)

Pacific Plate

Plate boundary

African Plate

Indian Plate

Australian Plate

Moving plates

Earth's crust is broken into seven large moving plates and many smaller ones. At the boundaries, where two plates meet, mountains or volcanoes form and earthquakes occur.

Human influence

More than half of Earth's 6.7 billion humans live in towns and cities, which take up less than five per cent of the planet's total land. Over the last 10,000 years, humans have destroyed nearly 25 per cent of the world's tree cover to provide farm land.

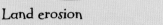

Land erosion

Wind, water, ice, and changing temperatures all alter Earth's landscape. Rivers and glaciers carve out valleys, ocean waves batter the coastline, and winds wear away rocks, resulting in distorted shapes.

Let me out!

Changing surface

Earth's surface has been changing since the planet's formation about 4.6 billion years ago. The oceans formed from steam in the young planet's atmosphere, which condensed into water droplets and fell to the surface. The land surface evolves continually through the forces of nature and also by human action.

Look out

This looks a tight squeeze

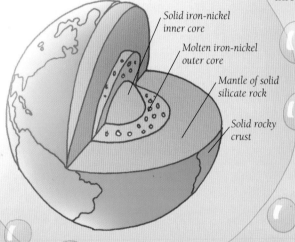

Solid iron-nickel inner core

Molten iron-nickel outer core

Mantle of solid silicate rock

Solid rocky crust

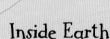

Surface features

Vast oceans of water, two polar ice caps, and continents of land, with mountainous and flatter regions, are all visible from Space. Green areas of land are forests and grasslands, but yellow-brown regions are mainly deserts.

That planet looks familiar...

I'm forever blowing bubbles

Inside Earth

Our planet is a ball of mainly rock and metal, loosely divided into layers. Following Earth's formation, the heavy metal sank to form a core and partially solidified as it cooled. Above its mantle of rock is a thin rocky crust that supports the oceans and land.

Pop!

Any more and you'll burst

HOME PLANET

We inhabit a unique planet. Earth's liquid water surface and variety of life forms are not found anywhere else in the Solar System. At 12,765 km (7,926 miles) in width, Earth is the largest rocky planet. Over time, oceans and atmosphere have formed, while movement and erosion have reshaped land masses. Our planet is third from the Sun. Earth orbits our star once a year, and spins as it travels, rotating every 23.9 hours.

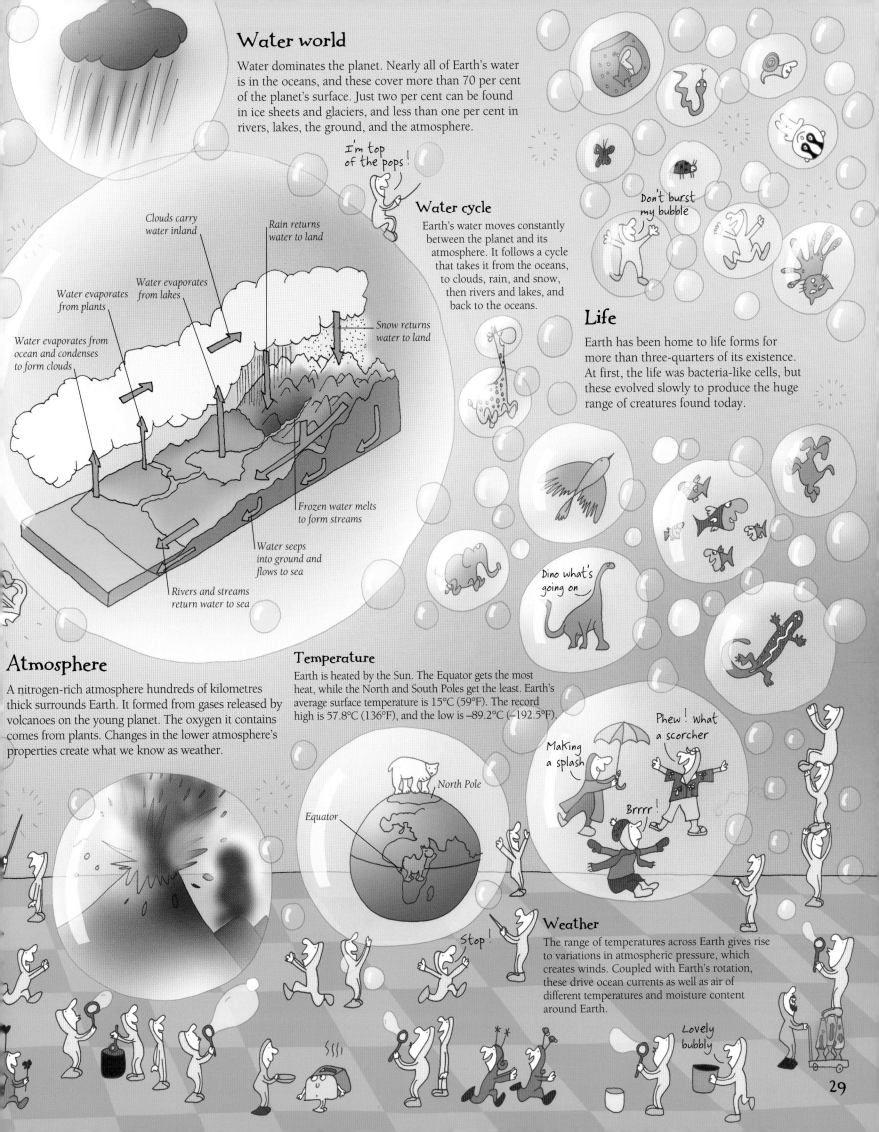

Water world

Water dominates the planet. Nearly all of Earth's water is in the oceans, and these cover more than 70 per cent of the planet's surface. Just two per cent can be found in ice sheets and glaciers, and less than one per cent in rivers, lakes, the ground, and the atmosphere.

Water cycle

Earth's water moves constantly between the planet and its atmosphere. It follows a cycle that takes it from the oceans, to clouds, rain, and snow, then rivers and lakes, and back to the oceans.

Clouds carry water inland

Rain returns water to land

Water evaporates from lakes

Water evaporates from plants

Snow returns water to land

Water evaporates from ocean and condenses to form clouds

Frozen water melts to form streams

Water seeps into ground and flows to sea

Rivers and streams return water to sea

Life

Earth has been home to life forms for more than three-quarters of its existence. At first, the life was bacteria-like cells, but these evolved slowly to produce the huge range of creatures found today.

Atmosphere

A nitrogen-rich atmosphere hundreds of kilometres thick surrounds Earth. It formed from gases released by volcanoes on the young planet. The oxygen it contains comes from plants. Changes in the lower atmosphere's properties create what we know as weather.

Temperature

Earth is heated by the Sun. The Equator gets the most heat, while the North and South Poles get the least. Earth's average surface temperature is 15°C (59°F). The record high is 57.8°C (136°F), and the low is −89.2°C (−192.5°F)

North Pole

Equator

Weather

The range of temperatures across Earth gives rise to variations in atmospheric pressure, which creates winds. Coupled with Earth's rotation, these drive ocean currents as well as air of different temperatures and moisture content around Earth.

Best mate Moon

The Moon is Earth's constant companion in Space. About a quarter of Earth's size, it orbits around our planet and travels with us as we make our yearly orbit of the Sun. It rotates in the same amount of time that it orbits Earth, and as a result, the same face of the Moon is kept towards us at all times. The shine is caused by reflected light from the Sun. This dry, dead ball of rock is the only other world where humans have walked.

Moonwatching

Easy to spot, the Moon is the largest Space body in Earth's night sky. The dark, flat areas visible on the surface looked like seas to early observers, and they mistakenly called them "maria" (Latin for "seas"). Lighter areas are older, higher rocks.

Lunar-tic

I'm getting cheesed off

Don't Brie like that

PHASES OF THE MOON

Last quarter

Waning crescent

Waning gibbous

New Moon

Full Moon

Waxing crescent

Waxing gibbous

First quarter

Don't be catty!

It's barking to let dogs in

Phases of the Moon

The Moon appears to change shape because of the varying amounts of sunlight on its face. It is sometimes fully lit by the Sun, sometimes partially lit, and at other times has no light at all. These changing shapes are its phases; a complete cycle takes 29.5 days.

Are you ok?

It's just a phase I'm going through

Eclipse of the Moon

When Earth is directly between the Sun and the Moon, it stops sunlight reaching the Moon. When the Moon is in Earth's shadow, it is eclipsed. It doesn't disappear from view but takes on a reddish glow due to the scattering of sunlight as it passes through Earth's atmosphere.

Moon is totally eclipsed

Umbra is the inner shadow

Earth

Penumbra is the outer shadow

Sunlight

Sun

I've got the weight of the world

Nearly done?

Pass the sunblock

I hear you are a big cheese

Moon myths

Many cultures have stories associated with the Moon. Some believe the full Moon has the power to turn people mad or transform them into hairy, scary werewolves. Others suggest the Moon is made of cheese, or explain a lunar eclipse as an animal temporarily swallowing the Moon!

Witch Flavour is this?

I'm wolfing it down

Devilishly tasty

Is this a mousetrap?

Birth of the Moon

The Moon formed about 4.5 billion years ago when a Mars-sized asteroid gave the young Earth a big blow. Material from the asteroid and Earth flung into Space and formed a ring around our planet. The material eventually came together and formed one body, the Moon.

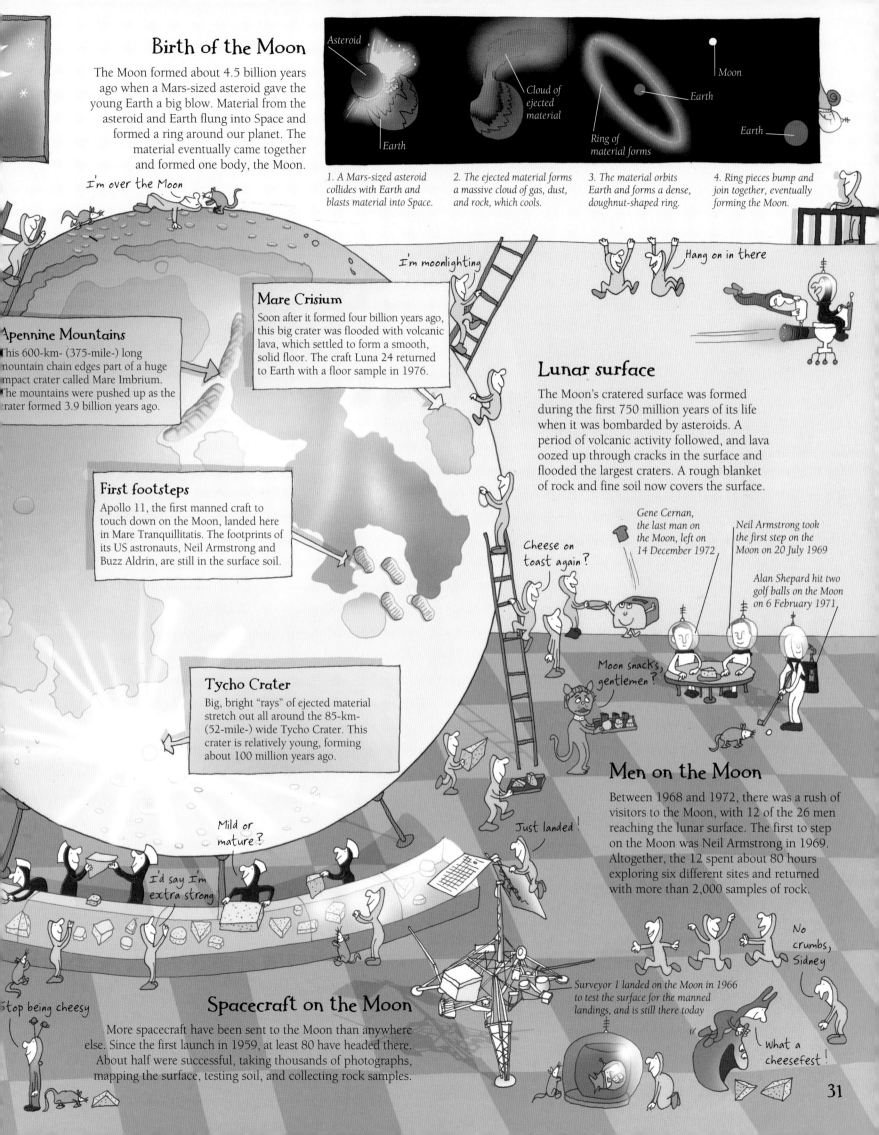

Asteroid

Earth

Cloud of ejected material

Moon

Earth

Ring of material forms

Earth

1. A Mars-sized asteroid collides with Earth and blasts material into Space.

2. The ejected material forms a massive cloud of gas, dust, and rock, which cools.

3. The material orbits Earth and forms a dense, doughnut-shaped ring.

4. Ring pieces bump and join together, eventually forming the Moon.

I'm over the Moon

I'm moonlighting

Hang on in there

Mare Crisium

Soon after it formed four billion years ago, this big crater was flooded with volcanic lava, which settled to form a smooth, solid floor. The craft Luna 24 returned to Earth with a floor sample in 1976.

Apennine Mountains

This 600-km- (375-mile-) long mountain chain edges part of a huge impact crater called Mare Imbrium. The mountains were pushed up as the crater formed 3.9 billion years ago.

Lunar surface

The Moon's cratered surface was formed during the first 750 million years of its life when it was bombarded by asteroids. A period of volcanic activity followed, and lava oozed up through cracks in the surface and flooded the largest craters. A rough blanket of rock and fine soil now covers the surface.

First footsteps

Apollo 11, the first manned craft to touch down on the Moon, landed here in Mare Tranquillitatis. The footprints of its US astronauts, Neil Armstrong and Buzz Aldrin, are still in the surface soil.

Gene Cernan, the last man on the Moon, left on 14 December 1972

Neil Armstrong took the first step on the Moon on 20 July 1969

Cheese on toast again?

Alan Shepard hit two golf balls on the Moon on 6 February 1971

Moon snacks, gentlemen?

Tycho Crater

Big, bright "rays" of ejected material stretch out all around the 85-km- (52-mile-) wide Tycho Crater. This crater is relatively young, forming about 100 million years ago.

Men on the Moon

Between 1968 and 1972, there was a rush of visitors to the Moon, with 12 of the 26 men reaching the lunar surface. The first to step on the Moon was Neil Armstrong in 1969. Altogether, the 12 spent about 80 hours exploring six different sites and returned with more than 2,000 samples of rock.

Mild or mature?

Just landed!

I'd say I'm extra strong

No crumbs, Sidney

Stop being cheesy

Spacecraft on the Moon

More spacecraft have been sent to the Moon than anywhere else. Since the first launch in 1959, at least 80 have headed there. About half were successful, taking thousands of photographs, mapping the surface, testing soil, and collecting rock samples.

Surveyor 1 landed on the Moon in 1966 to test the surface for the manned landings, and is still there today

What a cheesefest!

31

On the surface

Mercury's surface is covered by impact craters. Most date from when the planet was bombarded by asteroids more than 3.5 billion years ago. They range from small bowl-shaped ones to the Caloris Basin, which covers a quarter of the planet. A thin, temporary atmosphere neither shields the surface, nor hangs on to its heat.

Temperature range

Mercury has the greatest temperature range of all the Solar System planets. During the day, the temperature rises to 430°C (806°F). At night, the heat is lost and the temperature plummets to −180°C (−356°F).

Impact craters

Mercury's craters formed when fast-moving asteroids hit the planet's surface and blasted out circular-shaped hollows. Surface rock was crushed and thrown in all directions, producing the dusty soil-like layer that covers Mercury today.

Hot spot

The Caloris Basin is one of the hottest spots on Mercury. It was formed four billion years ago by a 100-km-(62-mile-) wide asteroid. The shockwaves from the impact were so intense they even shattered the opposite side of the planet's surface.

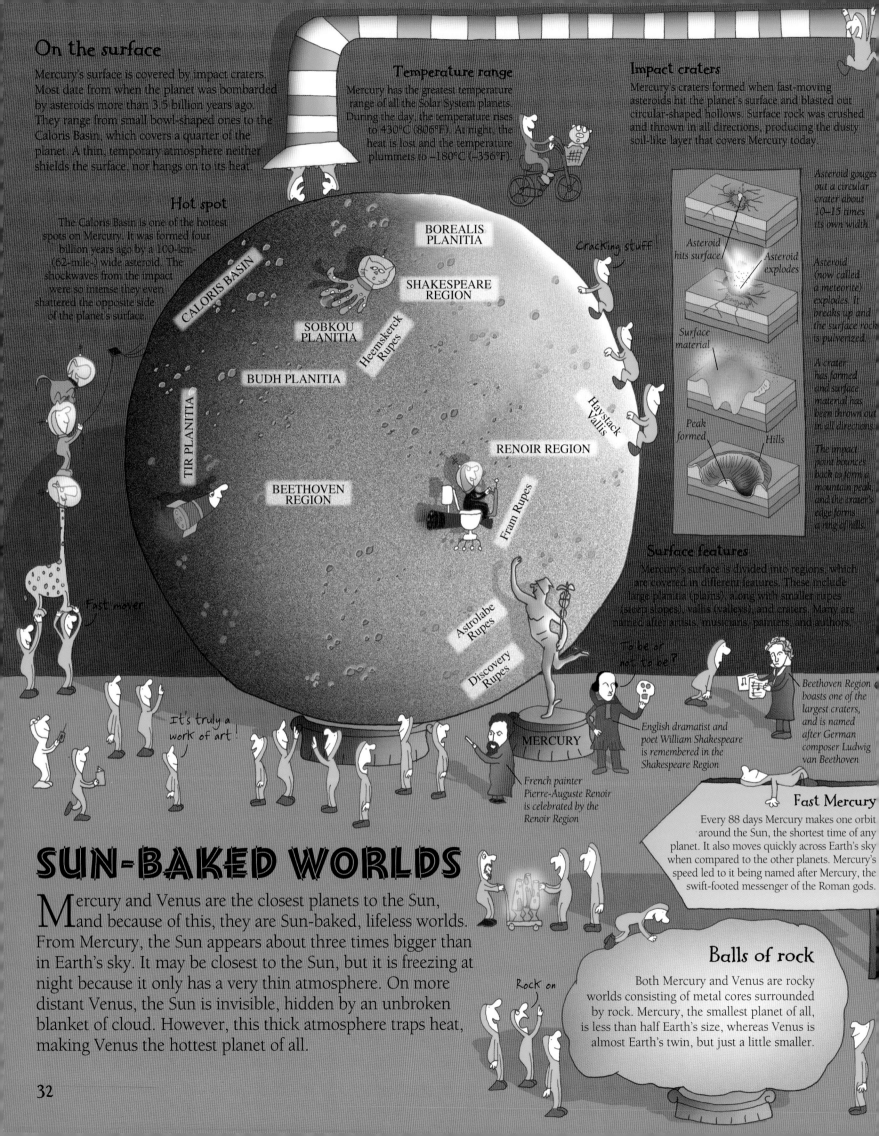

Asteroid gouges out a circular crater about 10–15 times its own width.

Asteroid hits surface

Asteroid explodes

Asteroid (now called a meteorite) explodes. It breaks up and the surface rock is pulverized.

Surface material

A crater has formed and surface material has been thrown out in all directions.

Peak formed

Hills

The impact point bounces back to form a mountain peak, and the crater's edge forms a ring of hills.

Cracking stuff!

BOREALIS PLANITIA

SHAKESPEARE REGION

CALORIS BASIN

SOBKOU PLANITIA

Heemskerck Rupes

BUDH PLANITIA

Haystack Vallis

TIR PLANITIA

RENOIR REGION

BEETHOVEN REGION

Fram Rupes

Astrolabe Rupes

Discovery Rupes

Fast mover

Surface features

Mercury's surface is divided into regions, which are covered in different features. These include large planitia (plains) along with smaller rupes (steep slopes), vallis (valleys), and craters. Many are named after artists, musicians, painters, and authors.

To be or not to be?

English dramatist and poet William Shakespeare is remembered in the Shakespeare Region

Beethoven Region boasts one of the largest craters, and is named after German composer Ludwig van Beethoven

It's truly a work of art!

MERCURY

French painter Pierre-Auguste Renoir is celebrated by the Renoir Region

Fast Mercury

Every 88 days Mercury makes one orbit around the Sun, the shortest time of any planet. It also moves quickly across Earth's sky when compared to the other planets. Mercury's speed led to it being named after Mercury, the swift-footed messenger of the Roman gods.

SUN-BAKED WORLDS

Mercury and Venus are the closest planets to the Sun, and because of this, they are Sun-baked, lifeless worlds. From Mercury, the Sun appears about three times bigger than in Earth's sky. It may be closest to the Sun, but it is freezing at night because it only has a very thin atmosphere. On more distant Venus, the Sun is invisible, hidden by an unbroken blanket of cloud. However, this thick atmosphere traps heat, making Venus the hottest planet of all.

Rock on

Balls of rock

Both Mercury and Venus are rocky worlds consisting of metal cores surrounded by rock. Mercury, the smallest planet of all, is less than half Earth's size, whereas Venus is almost Earth's twin, but just a little smaller.

Hot, hot, hot

Venus is a scorching, suffocating, gloomy world. It is almost twice as far from the Sun as Mercury, but much hotter. Under the clouds that cover the entire planet, its temperature is an almost constant 464°C (867°F). This varies by only a few degrees from day to night, and across the planet.

Thick atmosphere

A carbon-dioxide-rich atmosphere reaches up about 80 km (50 miles) from the ground. It contains a thick deck of clouds made of sulphuric acid droplets. They reflect about 80 per cent of the Sun's light back into Space, making Venus's surface overcast and murky.

Sunlight

Cloud

Ground heat

Greenhouse effect

Venus's cloud deck works like the glass in a greenhouse, trapping heat in. The portion of sunlight that reaches Venus's surface warms the rock. Once this heat is released, it cannot escape, adding to the warming process.

Beautiful Venus

Sunlight reflected back into Space by Venus's clouds makes the planet shine brightly. Easy to see, it appears as a beautiful, bright object in Earth's sky. For this reason the planet was named after Venus, the Roman goddess of love and beauty. It makes one orbit of the Sun every 225 days.

ATALANTA PLANITIA

VELLAMO PLANITIA

VINMARA PLANITIA

Fornax Rupes

ATLA REGION

Diana and Dali Chasma are deep splits in the planet's surface

RUSALKA PLANITIA

Diana Chasma

Dali Chasma

Maat Mons is the tallest volcano, rising about 5 km (3 miles) above the surrounding land

Volcanoes

More than three-quarters of Venus's surface is low-lying plain consisting of vast areas of volcanic lava. Hundreds of volcanoes dot the planet, from large shallow-sloped ones to small domes. The last eruptions were about 500 million years ago.

IMDR REGION

NSOMEKA PLANITIA

VENUS

I'm fishing for compliments

Hot stuff

Help

Guess I don't need a tan after all

Vicious Venus

Humans couldn't survive on Venus. They would be poisoned by its atmosphere, squashed by the surface pressure of its atmospheric gases, and cooked by its constant high temperature.

Woman's world

All but one of the surface features on Venus are named after women. They include goddesses, mythological heroines, famous historical women, and female first names.

I'm feeling the heat

She's a dangerous beauty!

Guinevere, a mythical English queen, gives her name to the largest plain on Venus (on the other side of the planet)

Freyja, the mythical Norse goddess known for her beauty is remembered in the name of a mountain range near the North Pole

Watch out, ladies!

He's over us

Love hurts

You're the real queen of my heart

Egyptian queen Cleopatra's impact crater is located in the planet's north

33

HOLIDAY ON MARS

Named after the Roman god of war, Mars is also known as the "red planet" because of its rusty red colour. This rocky planet is about half the size of Earth. It orbits the Sun every 687 days and spins on its axis every 24.6 hours so its day-length is similar to Earth's. The Martian surface is all rock, with ice layers at the two polar caps. Famous features include giant volcanoes, deep canyons, and two tiny moons.

Welcome to Mars!

Distance to Sun: 228 million km (140 million miles)

Population: 0

Outlook: Cold with a slight wind

Temperature: −63°C (−81°F)

Next train to Earth departing: 7.30pm

Time to Earth: Nine months

Mars is pretty lifeless

Atmosphere

Mars has a thin, carbon-dioxide atmosphere, which also contains fine particles of iron-oxide dust. The dust makes the atmosphere a pinky colour.

Seasons

Mars is tilted at an angle of about 25°. This means it experiences seasonal changes as its North Pole and South Pole take it in turns to point towards the Sun.

Weather

Mars is a dry world, with no rain clouds. However, there are occasional clouds of frozen carbon dioxide and ice. Winds can pick up surface dust and create powerful dust storms.

Temperature

Mars is further from the Sun than Earth, so it is a colder planet. The temperature here depends on your location and the season. It can range from −125°C (−193°F) to 25°C (77°F).

oh what an atmosphere...

It's the cat's whiskers

Purrrrrrrrr

Gravity

Mars's gravity is only about a third of Earth's. This means that you would weigh about two-thirds less than you do on Earth and you would be able to carry three times as much weight. The reduced gravity would make walking a struggle at first.

Monorail Cat is on time

That light lunch has paid off

Welcome to Mars!

Purrfect timing

Does it have a catalytic converter?

HISTORY DOME

where is the pool?

Wowsers! It's the Phoenix Lander!

Hmmm, doesn't do much though

That's gotta hurt

Space rocks

Mars has tens of thousands of craters on its surface. These formed when asteroids hit the planet more than 3.5 billion years ago. The smallest are about 0.5 km across and the largest are hundreds of kilometres wide.

You're a bit late

Wet past

When Mars was a young planet, about three billion years ago, it was a warmer and wetter world. Water flowed on its surface, forming lakes and seas inside craters. Today, Mars is dry with barren river beds and ancient floodplains.

Here, boy!

Past visitors

Mars has had fewer than 30 visitors in its entire history. All came from Earth and all were spacecraft. The first one flew by in 1964, while others have orbited the planet or landed on it, such as Mars Phoenix Lander in 2008.

Push off, pooch

North Polar Cap

Caps of ice cover the regions around Mars's North and South Poles. Layers of ice and dust stand several kilometres above the land surrounding the northern cap. In winter, it is permanently dark for about six months. Carbon-dioxide frost and snow then cover the water ice, but disappear in summer..

Phobos

Mars's two moons, Phobos and Deimos, are potato-shaped lumps of rock covered in craters. Originally asteroids, they were captured into orbits around Mars. About 27 km (16 miles) in length, Phobos is the larger moon, orbiting Mars every 7.5 hours. It rises and sets in the Martian sky three times a day.

Opportunity

Twin robot geologists arrived on opposite sides of Mars in 2004. Named Opportunity and Spirit, they have been driving across the surface, using tools and cameras to study rocks and soil. Opportunity has travelled more than 19 km (12 miles) while investigating craters and recording evidence of the planet's watery past.

Olympus Mons

The largest volcano in the whole of the Solar System is Olympus Mons. It is about 24 km (15 miles) in height and is named after the mountain-top home of the Ancient Greek gods. The volcano grew gradually as regular outpourings of molten rock flowed from its top many millions of years ago.

Valles Marineris

This system of canyons cuts across the centre of Mars. It formed 3.5 billion years ago when the planet's crust stretched and split. Winds and water have since lengthened the canyons to 4,000 km (2,485 miles) and deepened them to 8 km (5 miles).

RING OF RUBBLE

Billions of asteroids orbit the Sun. These chunky rocks were left over when the planets were made. Each asteroid follows its own orbit, but most are found in a doughnut-shaped region of Space between the orbits of Mars and Jupiter. Together they make up the Asteroid Belt, also called the Main Belt. Asteroids, or pieces of them, have landed on Earth's surface. When this happens, they are known as meteorites.

Asteroid profile

Most asteroids are dry, dusty rocks, but some are made of metal, or a mix of rock and metal. Nearly all are irregular lumps with cratered surfaces. The largest is Ceres, which is 938 km (583 miles) across and is also classed as a dwarf planet.

CERES

Trojans

Ceres

Shape and size

Only eight asteroids are bigger than 300 km (186 miles) in width, and these are spherical. Of the irregular-shaped ones, such as Ida, 100,000 are more than 20 km (12 miles) across, and a billion are more than 2 km (1 mile).

IDA

Orbit and spin

Asteroids usually take between four and five years to orbit the Sun. Each one spins as it orbits, taking just a few hours for one complete spin.

Keep up!

Keep pedalling

DRIVE-IN SNACKS

Once you pop, you can't stop

Very pop-ular

Asteroid names

Of more than 215,000 identified asteroids, 15,000 have been named. Astronomers who discover asteroids can name them. Most are named after people, such as the astronomers or their relatives, as well as writers, musicians, and fictional characters

James Bond (fictional spy)

I spy...

Cheshirecat (the cat in Lewis Carroll's Alice in Wonderland)

Miaow for now

I'm the magic man

Merlin (wizard of Arthurian legend)

Neigh he's not

Mr Spock (the discoverer's cat was named after this Star Trek character)

Harrison, Lennon, McCartney, and Starr – members of 1960s music group The Beatles

Must be the Rolling Stones

Main Belt

More than 90 per cent of asteroids can be found in the Main Belt. They are the remains of a planet that failed to form. It would have been about four times as massive as Earth, but Jupiter's gravity stopped the material producing one object.

Beyond the belt

Some asteroids orbit the Sun outside the Main Belt. These include the Trojans, found in two groups along Jupiter's orbit, and near-Earth asteroids, which were once in the Main Belt but now follow orbits that bring them closer to Earth.

Jupiter

Trojans

Earth

Apollo

Eros

Mars

Sun

Ida

Trojans

There are several thousand Trojans, and they take 11.8 years to orbit the Sun once, the same length of time as Jupiter. They exist in two swarms: one is 60 degrees in front of Jupiter, the other is 60 degrees behind it.

Near-Earth asteroids

These asteroids follow orbits that cross or approach Earth's orbit. This means they can pass relatively close to Earth or, in rare cases, hit our planet. Apollo and Eros are both near-Earth asteroids.

COMING SOON:
ASTEROID COLLISIONS!

CRATERING

Asteroid is less than 1/50,000th of size of larger asteroid

Crater forms

FRACTURING

Asteroid is 1/50,000th of size of larger asteroid

Asteroid fractures

Breaks into fragments

Forms ball of rubble

SHATTERING

Asteroid is more than 1/50,000th of size of larger asteroid

Larger asteroid shatters apart

Family of asteroids forms

Collisions

High-speed collisions occur between asteroids. Most involve a small asteroid forming an impact crater on a larger one. Asteroids can also fracture into pieces that come together again or shatter apart completely.

COMING SOON:
DEATH OF THE DINOSAURS!

Fall to Earth

More than 170 craters exist on Earth where asteroids have smashed into the planet. Chicxulub, off the coast of Mexico, is a crater that formed 65 million years ago. Material thrown up by the impact affected the atmosphere, which some think led to the dinosaurs dying out.

Stony-iron meteorite

Stony meteorite

Iron meteorite

Meteorites

About 3,000 pieces of asteroid, each weighing more than 1 kg (2 lb), fall on Earth's land or into its oceans every year. There are three main types: stony (making up 93 per cent of all meteorites), iron, and stony-iron.

That's meteor-wrong!

Stone me!

We're on a rocky road

Watch your gnashers!

Slurp!

Rock on!

GIANT PLANETS

The four outer planets are the largest in the Solar System and are mostly made of gas and liquid. Jupiter, Saturn, Uranus, and Neptune are all ice-cold worlds far beyond Earth. Each has a ring system and a large family of moons. When we look at these giant planets, we see the tops of their colourful gas atmospheres, leading some to call them the "gas giants".

Planetary profile

The density and temperature of the materials the planets are made of increases with depth. This affects the physical state of the material. For instance, Jupiter is mostly hydrogen over a rocky core. Below its atmosphere, the gas gradually becomes liquid, and deep down is like a molten metal.

Jupiter

This planet is the Solar System's record breaker. It is the biggest and most massive planet, and because it takes less than ten hours to rotate, it is also the fastest spinner. It is made of two and a half times the material of the other seven planets combined.

What a big boy!

Jupiter is so huge that 11 Earths could fit across it, and 1,300 inside it

Great Red Spot, a giant storm bigger than Earth

Jupiter takes 12 years to travel once around the Sun

Stormy weather

All four giants have weather systems in their atmospheres, but Jupiter's is the most visible. The planet's fast spin helps pull its clouds into red-brown and white striped bands parallel to its equator. Spots on Jupiter's visible surface are giant weather storms.

Saturn

None of the giants is a perfect sphere. They are all oblate like squashed balls – wider around their equators than from top to bottom. Saturn is the most oblate. It is also the least dense planet, and because of this, it would float if placed in water.

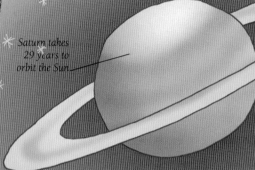

Saturn takes 29 years to orbit the Sun

Rings are made of thousands of individual ice pieces, each orbiting the planet

Ring leader

All of the giants have rings, but Saturn's are the most extensive and spectacular. It has seven separate rings, each made of hundreds of ringlets. These are made of pieces of dirty water ice ranging in size from dust grains to large boulders.

Families of moons

All but three of the moons that orbit Solar System planets spin around a giant planet. Jupiter and Saturn have the largest families, with more than 60 moons each. Jupiter's moon Ganymede is the largest moon – it is bigger than the planet Mercury.

Io, the most volcanic place in the Solar System

It's Titanic!

Titan

Saturn's largest moon is Titan, and it is the only moon of any planet to have a substantial atmosphere. It is also the only moon that a spacecraft has landed on apart from Earth's Moon.

Shepherd moons

Each of the giants has irregularly-shaped moons ranging in size from a few to a few hundred kilometres across. These include some within Saturn's rings that shepherd the ring particles into position.

Gutterball

Galilean moons

I cut a striking figure

Jupiter's four largest moons are known as the Galilean moons after the astronomer Galileo Galilei. Ganymede, Callisto, and Europa are icy, but Io is a volcanic world.

King of the gods

The biggest planet is named after Jupiter, king of the Roman gods and ruler of the heavens. He controlled storms, and all land struck by lightning was his.

I'm the greatest

Supreme ruler

Planet Saturn is named after the one-time ruler of all the Roman gods, who was overthrown by his son Jupiter.

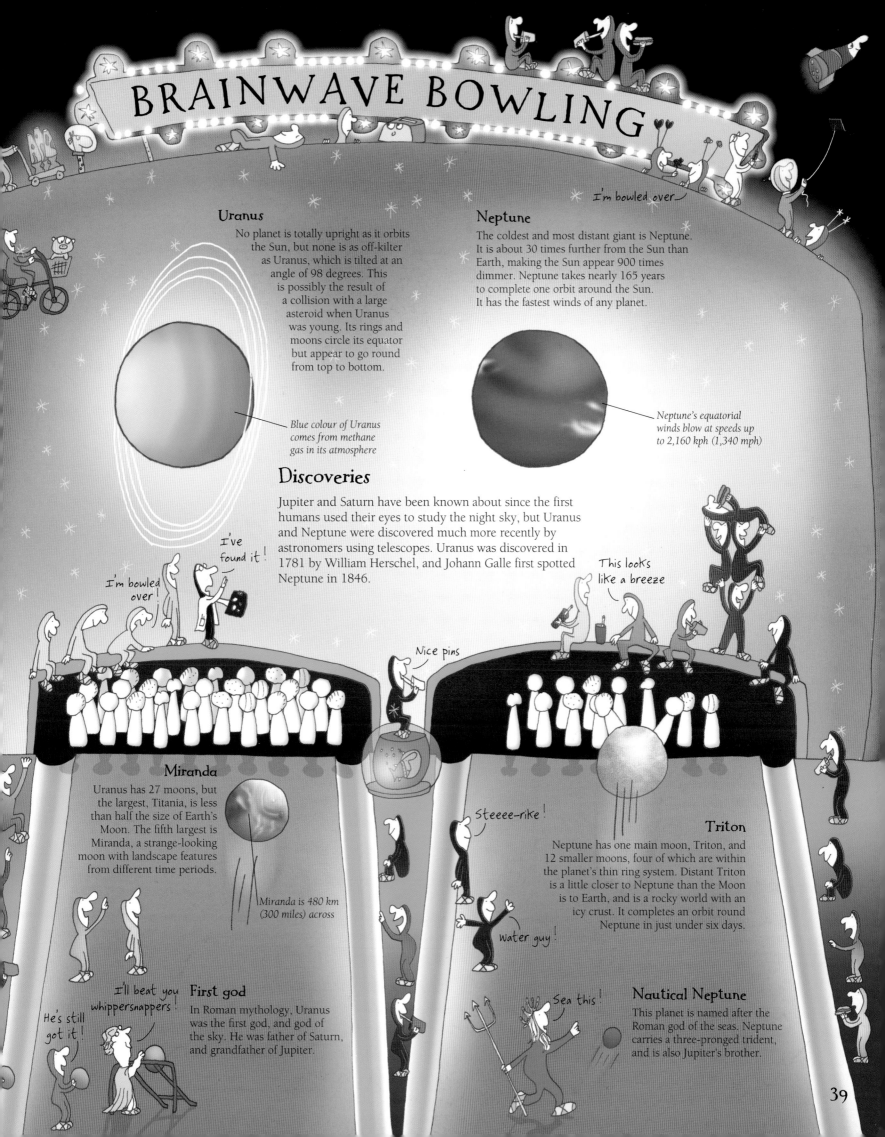

BRAINWAVE BOWLING

Uranus

No planet is totally upright as it orbits the Sun, but none is as off-kilter as Uranus, which is tilted at an angle of 98 degrees. This is possibly the result of a collision with a large asteroid when Uranus was young. Its rings and moons circle its equator but appear to go round from top to bottom.

Blue colour of Uranus comes from methane gas in its atmosphere

Neptune

The coldest and most distant giant is Neptune. It is about 30 times further from the Sun than Earth, making the Sun appear 900 times dimmer. Neptune takes nearly 165 years to complete one orbit around the Sun. It has the fastest winds of any planet.

Neptune's equatorial winds blow at speeds up to 2,160 kph (1,340 mph)

Discoveries

Jupiter and Saturn have been known about since the first humans used their eyes to study the night sky, but Uranus and Neptune were discovered much more recently by astronomers using telescopes. Uranus was discovered in 1781 by William Herschel, and Johann Galle first spotted Neptune in 1846.

Miranda

Uranus has 27 moons, but the largest, Titania, is less than half the size of Earth's Moon. The fifth largest is Miranda, a strange-looking moon with landscape features from different time periods.

Miranda is 480 km (300 miles) across

First god

In Roman mythology, Uranus was the first god, and god of the sky. He was father of Saturn, and grandfather of Jupiter.

Triton

Neptune has one main moon, Triton, and 12 smaller moons, four of which are within the planet's thin ring system. Distant Triton is a little closer to Neptune than the Moon is to Earth, and is a rocky world with an icy crust. It completes an orbit round Neptune in just under six days.

Nautical Neptune

This planet is named after the Roman god of the seas. Neptune carries a three-pronged trident, and is also Jupiter's brother.

39

Frozen worlds

There are trillions of comets in the freezing outer reaches of the Solar System. They are huge dirty snowballs that have remained unchanged since the Sun and planets formed 4.6 billion years ago. Occasionally, one travels closer to the Sun, and this changes its size and appearance. Many other small worlds of ice and rock live in a flattened ring beyond Neptune, known as the Kuiper Belt.

Comet characteristics

All comets consist of a giant snowball called a nucleus. Each is the width of a big city. Comets travelling close to the Sun become tens of thousands of times larger when they develop a vast head and tails.

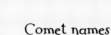

Coma, typically 100,000 km (62,000 miles) in width

Nucleus

Dust tail

Gas tail

Tails

Gas and dust released from the nucleus by the Sun's heat form two tails millions of kilometres long. The gas tail is straight and blue-white; the dust one is curved and white.

Nucleus

The nucleus is irregular in shape and is a mix of two-thirds snow and one-third rock dust. A thin layer of dust covers its surface.

Coma

A huge head called a coma is made of gas and dust. It forms when the Sun's heat turns the snow on the surface of the nucleus into gas, and loosens dust in the process.

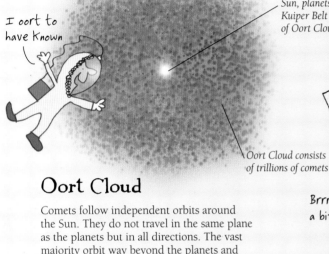

Sun, planets, and Kuiper Belt in centre of Oort Cloud

I oort to have known

Oort Cloud consists of trillions of comets

Oort Cloud

Comets follow independent orbits around the Sun. They do not travel in the same plane as the planets but in all directions. The vast majority orbit way beyond the planets and together make a large sphere of comets called the Oort Cloud.

Steady on, Sidney!

Don't give me the cold shoulder

RACE START

On your marks... get set... go!

Whooooosh!

Brrr! It's a bit nippy

Come on, comet!

Comet names

New discoveries are routinely called after the discoverer's family name. When two astronomers discover one comet independently, it is given both their names, for instance, Hale-Bopp. Occasionally three discoverers are included.

Great comets

Comet McNaught, 2007 – discovered 7 August 2006 by Scotsman Robert McNaught
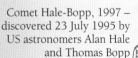

Comet Hale-Bopp, 1997 – discovered 23 July 1995 by US astronomers Alan Hale and Thomas Bopp
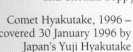

Comet Hyakutake, 1996 – discovered 30 January 1996 by Japan's Yuji Hyakutake

Comet Bennett, 1970 – discovered 28 December 1969 by South African John Bennett

Kuiper Belt

About a thousand icy rock bodies called Kuiper Belt Objects have been identified beyond Neptune. They orbit the Sun as part of the Kuiper Belt, which is believed to consist of many more such objects. The belt also contains some comets and a few dwarf planets.

Pluto was classed as a planet from its discovery in 1930 until 2006, when it was re-classed as a dwarf planet

Dwarf planets

The largest objects in the Kuiper Belt are almost round, planet-like objects called dwarf planets, such as Eris and Pluto. Astronomers introduced the class of dwarf planets in 2006.

You're the greatest

I'm ready for comet-ment!

I see a rocky road ahead

I can run rings around you!

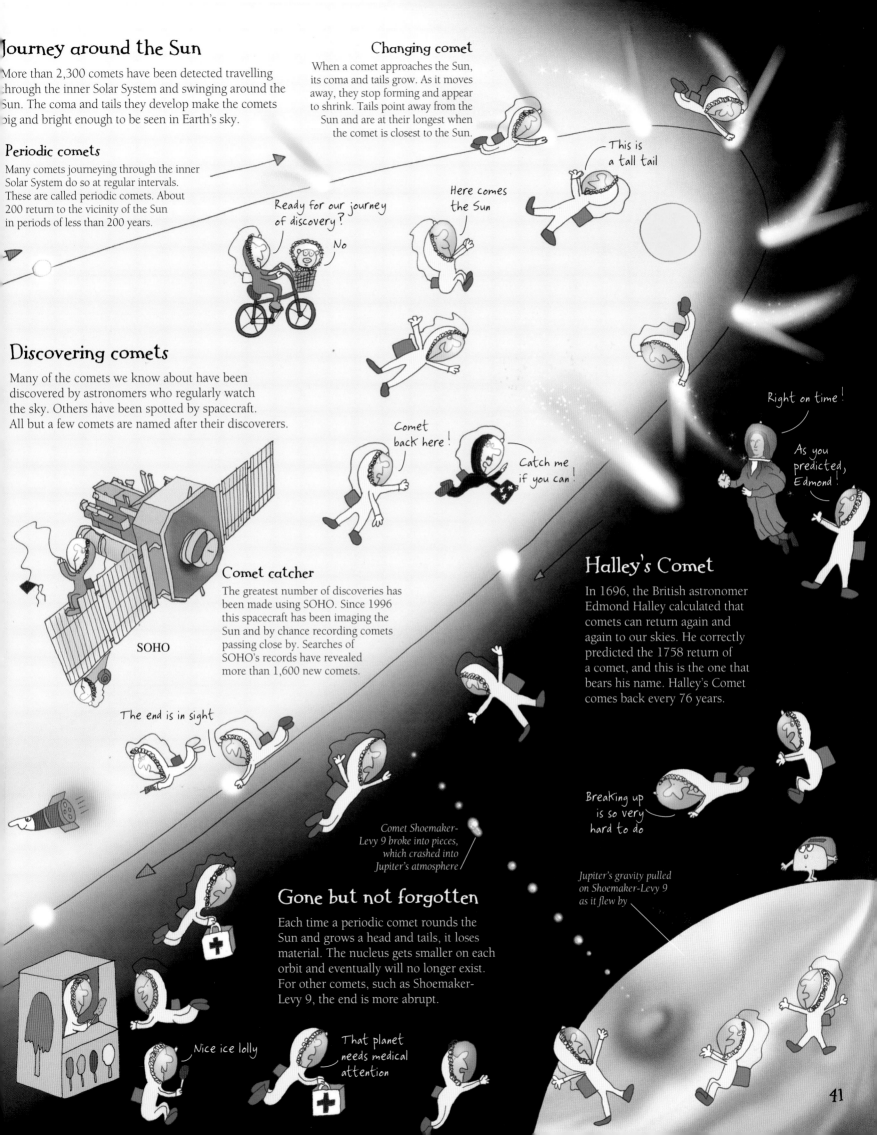

Journey around the Sun

More than 2,300 comets have been detected travelling through the inner Solar System and swinging around the Sun. The coma and tails they develop make the comets big and bright enough to be seen in Earth's sky.

Periodic comets

Many comets journeying through the inner Solar System do so at regular intervals. These are called periodic comets. About 200 return to the vicinity of the Sun in periods of less than 200 years.

Discovering comets

Many of the comets we know about have been discovered by astronomers who regularly watch the sky. Others have been spotted by spacecraft. All but a few comets are named after their discoverers.

SOHO

Comet catcher

The greatest number of discoveries has been made using SOHO. Since 1996 this spacecraft has been imaging the Sun and by chance recording comets passing close by. Searches of SOHO's records have revealed more than 1,600 new comets.

The end is in sight

Changing comet

When a comet approaches the Sun, its coma and tails grow. As it moves away, they stop forming and appear to shrink. Tails point away from the Sun and are at their longest when the comet is closest to the Sun.

This is a tall tail

Here comes the Sun

Ready for our journey of discovery?

No

Comet back here!

Catch me if you can!

Halley's Comet

In 1696, the British astronomer Edmond Halley calculated that comets can return again and again to our skies. He correctly predicted the 1758 return of a comet, and this is the one that bears his name. Halley's Comet comes back every 76 years.

Right on time!

As you predicted, Edmond!

Breaking up is so very hard to do

Gone but not forgotten

Each time a periodic comet rounds the Sun and grows a head and tails, it loses material. The nucleus gets smaller on each orbit and eventually will no longer exist. For other comets, such as Shoemaker-Levy 9, the end is more abrupt.

Comet Shoemaker-Levy 9 broke into pieces, which crashed into Jupiter's atmosphere

Jupiter's gravity pulled on Shoemaker-Levy 9 as it flew by

Nice ice lolly

That planet needs medical attention

Welcome to Space

Target Space

There is no natural barrier between Earth's atmosphere and Space, and because of this, not everyone agrees where Space starts. Astronauts are said to have travelled into Space once they reach 100 km (62 miles) above Earth. They feel weightless within ten minutes, but moving into orbit takes about an hour.

This is bad timing

Take a load off

Payload

Inside the nose of the rocket is the payload. This can be satellites for Earth orbit; a spacecraft journeying on to a planet; or a capsule with astronauts heading for the International Space Station.

Big nose!

Ouch

Room for a small one?

Take a load off

First of the rocket's two satellites to be released

Second-stage engine will ignite in Space, lifting the payload of two satellites into orbit

A satellite is inside this casing

That's a booster

You really rocket my world

Rocket stages

Space rockets usually consist of a number of parts, or stages, each with its own engine and fuel. When one completes its work, it is cast off. The first stage lifts the entire rocket off the ground. The second climbs higher still, and then releases the payload into orbit.

Payload is released into orbit

Second-stage engines fire

Second stage falls away

First stage drops away

Engines of first stage launch rocket off the ground

Astronaut return

Robotic craft do not need to return to Earth, but astronauts do. Those coming home from the International Space Station can return in a Soyuz craft, which splits to allow a crewed module to descend through Earth's atmosphere.

Parachutes slow the astronaut's descent through Earth's atmosphere

SpaceShipOne

In 2004, a privately owned spacecraft, SpaceShipOne, won a competition to find a reusable piloted craft that could travel to 100 km (62 miles) above Earth. It is carried to 15 km (9 miles) above Earth by the White Knight aircraft before being released to continue its journey.

SpaceShipOne is carried by White Knight

Edge of Space

On release, SpaceShipOne ignites its rocket engine, which powers the craft upwards to the edge of Space. Its wings slow its descent back to Earth, and the craft glides home.

Boiiiing!

Space shuttle system

Conventional rockets are used only once, but the space shuttle is a reusable launch craft. It launches like a rocket but returns to Earth like a glider plane. The shuttle system has three main parts. These are the orbiter, the fuel tank for the orbiter's engines, and the booster rockets.

Fuel tank is used only once, and when empty it falls back to Earth, breaking up over the ocean

Booster rockets fall back to Earth, where they are collected and re-used

Orbiter

Orbiter fleet

The only part of the shuttle that goes into Space is the orbiter, which carries a crew and payload. The remaining three orbiters – Discovery, Atlantis, and Endeavour – have made about 90 flights in all.

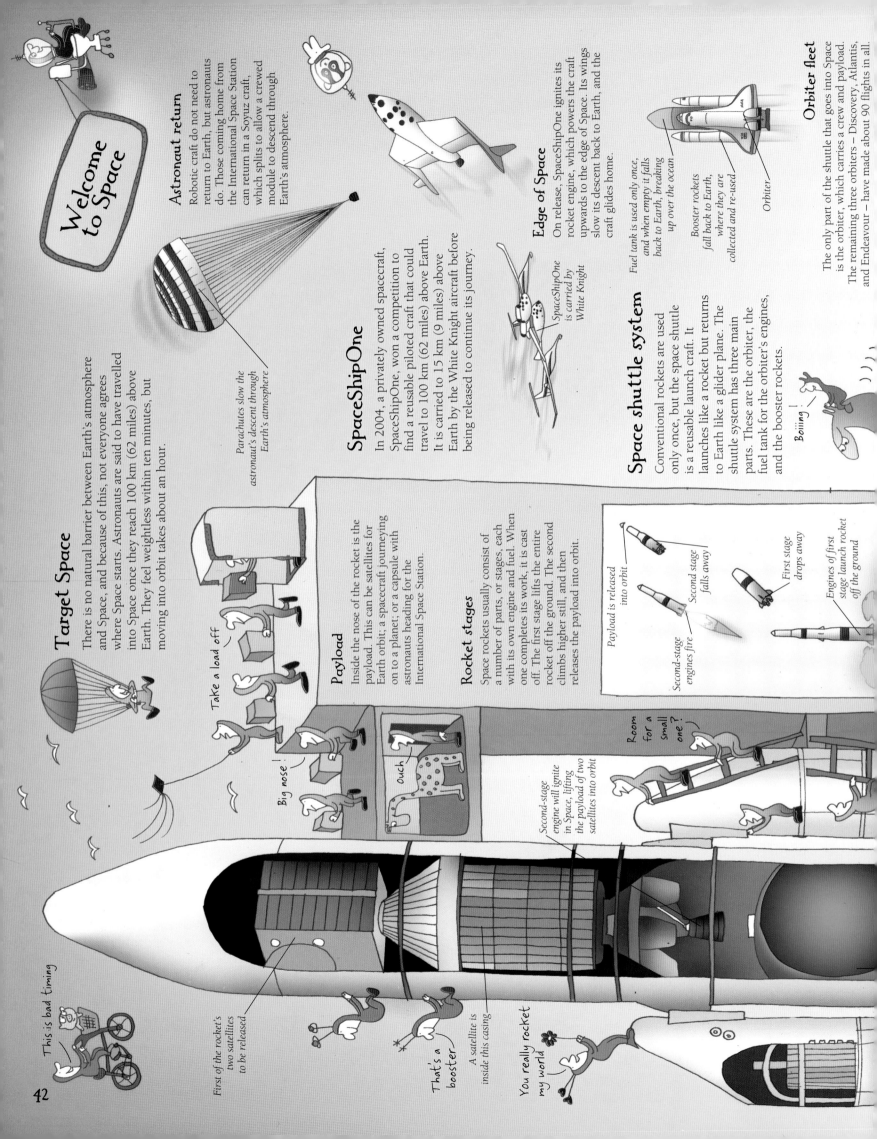

Shuttle return

Once back in Earth's atmosphere, air flows over the orbiter and its wings glide the craft towards the ground. Brakes, a rudder, and the wing edges slow the orbiter down, and once on the runway a drag chute brings it to a complete stop.

We've missed you!

Blast off

Rockets have been lifting off from Earth and heading for Space for more than 60 years. Today, about two rockets a week are launched, involving people from all around the world. Some nations launch rockets, but more send craft or astronauts into Space, or work as part of a global team monitoring a mission.

Launch site

There are about 30 rocket launch sites around Earth. Rockets launched from close to Earth's equator benefit from an extra push that the planet's spin gives them as they take off.

Ready for launch!

Did someone say lunch?

Control room

A launch is managed from a control room built safely away from the rocket. Once the final checks have been made, and the craft is declared ready for launch, the engines are ignited and the final countdown begins.

I'm in total control

I haven't had breakfast yet, never mind lunch

Escape velocity

Off the ground, a rocket speeds up quickly. If it goes too slowly, it falls back. It must reach about 11 km (7 miles) per second, called escape velocity. The rocket can then leave Earth's gravity for good.

Rocket is forced upwards, in the opposite direction to the movement of the gas

Rocket fuel

Gas produced by rocket fuel is forced out of the bottom of the rocket

Upward movement of rocket

Downward movement of gases

Rocket science

The three main parts of a rocket are its engine, fuel, and body. The fuel and engine provide thrust to carry the rocket upwards. Fuel burned in the engine produces gases that rush out of the rocket at high speed. The gases go down and force the rocket up.

Booster rockets

The hardest part of a rocket's job is lifting off the ground. At this time the rocket is at its heaviest because it consists of the rocket, its payload, and full fuel tanks. Booster rockets attached to the outside help by producing extra thrust.

This fuel tank contains liquid oxygen, which is mixed with the liquid hydrogen and ignited to power the rocket's first stage

Fuel tank has two compartments, this one contains liquid hydrogen

Gases forced through the engine's exhaust nozzle provide the thrust to lift rocket off the ground

10–9–8–7–6...

Ready for launch

For anything to leave Earth and travel into Space, a rocket is required. The power of the rocket lifts it off the ground and achieves the necessary speed to get away from the pull of Earth's gravity. Within a short time the rocket's job is complete. It has delivered its cargo, known as the payload, into Space, and it is now the payload's turn to start work.

Start the countdown

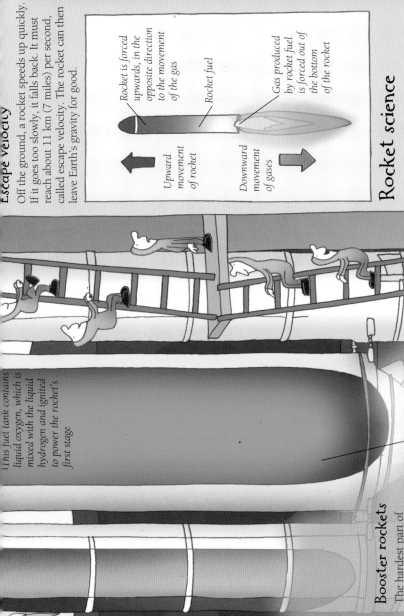

SPACE EXPLORERS SHOWROOM

Mission types

The craft perform one mission or a combination of different types. Fly-by craft investigate their target as they travel past, orbiters go around it, and landers touch-down on it. A small craft can hitch a ride on a larger one. On arrival, the smaller one is released to probe an atmosphere or explore a landscape.

Which way to the bargain basement?

On a wing and a prayer

Uranus

Neptune

VOYAGER 2

Can I come, too?

Behave, Sidney!

Escalating danger!

Voyager 2

The Voyager 2 craft made a grand tour of the giant planets. It flew by Jupiter, Saturn, Uranus, and Neptune between 1979 and 1989. Voyager 2 is currently heading away from the Sun.

Philae

ROSETTA

Rosetta

In 2015, on completion of a ten-year journey, the Rosetta craft will arrive near a comet and release Philae, a lander, onto its surface. Rosetta will orbit the comet as it travels on its journey around the Sun.

You gotta move with the times

LATEST MODEL!

Sojourner

Five rovers have been into Space, two have gone to the Moon, and three have visited Mars. The first to Mars was a microwave-oven-sized buggy called Sojourner. It worked for almost three months in 1997.

SOJOURNER

Mission target

Robot explorers have been to all eight planets, Earth's Moon, a small number of asteroids and comets, and approached the Sun. Some are still collecting data to send to Earth, while others have completed their missions. Though switched off, these craft continue to travel through Space or remain where they last landed.

No room for spacehoppers

Not you again!

Is our love on the up?

ROBOT EXPLORERS

Automated robotic spacecraft are sent from Earth to explore the Solar System. About the size of a bus or family car, they have a central body with equipment attached. Power is supplied by solar panels or nuclear fuel, a computer acts as the brain, small thruster rockets provide path adjustment, and tools of the trade can include cameras, heat sensors, and dust collectors. Designed for specific missions, the craft record their findings and transmit the results back to Earth.

RECENT SUCCESSES

GALILEO

Galileo studied Jupiter and moons from 1995 until 2003

MARS EXPRESS

This craft has been orbiting Mars since 2003

MAGELLAN

NEAR SHOEMAKER

Near Shoemaker landed on the asteroid Eros in 2001

Magellan mapped Venus from 1990 until 1994

SHOWROOM 1ST FLOOR

Let's get on with the show

Lunokhod 1

The first rover craft was Lunokhod 1. It explored the Moon for about ten months from November 1970. A twin craft Lunokhod 2 explored another part of the Moon in 1973.

VINTAGE CLASSIC!

LUNOKHOD 1

It's a bit dusty

Titan, Saturn's largest moon

Huygens

WORKSHOP THIS WAY

Cassini-Huygens

One of the largest and most complex craft ever built, Cassini-Huygens arrived at Saturn in 2004. Cassini moved into orbit around Saturn before releasing Huygens to parachute to Titan's surface.

STARDUST

CASSINI

Stardust

Occasionally, a mission returns with a sample. Three luna craft brought back Moon soil in the 1970s, while Stardust carried comet particles in 2006.

It's definitely old school

I'm a rover, too

No time for slackers

All work and no play...boo

Robot parts

The various parts of a craft are manufactured individually and then fixed together. New Horizons, the first mission to Pluto, was assembled by May 2005 for its January 2006 launch. It will arrive at Pluto in 2015 and fly past this dwarf planet before heading into the Kuiper Belt.

Antenna

Communication between Earth and New Horizons goes through its 2.1-m (6.8-ft) dish antenna.

How does it fit?

No idea

Instruments

PEPSSI (shown right) will measure material escaping from Pluto's atmosphere, and SWAP (shown left) will study Pluto's action with the solar wind.

NEW HORIZONS

Camera

LORRI is a telescopic camera that will provide images of Pluto from long distance.

Snap happy!

Atmosphere analyser

Component Alice will analyse the composition and structure of Pluto's atmosphere.

Names in Space

On board New Horizons are nine mementos of Earth, including photographs of the New Horizons team; a US postage stamp; a container of ashes of Clyde Tombaugh (discoverer of Pluto); and a compact disc with the names of 434,738 people on Earth.

Dust detector

Dust encountered by New Horizons as it travels to Pluto will be measured by Venetia.

Map maker

Component Ralph will provide colour, composition, and thermal (heat) maps of Pluto.

What's the name of the game?

I'm going to make a name for myself

You've spelt it wrong though

My name is going into Space!

Mission to Pluto

New Horizons keeps in contact through a series of huge antenna dishes based in Australia, Spain, and the USA. As Earth rotates, one dish is always in touch with the craft. Radio waves take 4.5 hours to arrive from Pluto.

Very dishy

What's new on Pluto?

Keeping in touch

Craft are pre-programmed to perform tasks at different times on each mission. A control team on Earth monitors a craft's progress, and sends instructions if plans need to change. Data collected by the craft is downloaded to Earth and forwarded on to astronomers.

The robot wishes we were there... bless him!

Send him my love and come back soon

Is it mission impossible?

No, it's mission accomplished

Space tourists

Six private citizens have paid about $25 million each for a week's stay on the International Space Station. The first was US businessman Dennis Tito in 2001. Like him, the other Space tourists travelled there and back by Soyuz rocket. One of the tourists, Hungarian-born Charles Simonyi, returned for a second stay in 2009.

Ticket to ride

The first privately designed and owned spacecraft will soon carry tourists into Space. On 21 June 2004, SpaceShipOne made the first privately funded human spaceflight. Seats aboard its successor can now be reserved. For $200,000, passengers get three days of pre-flight preparation, followed by six minutes of weightlessness on an edge-of-Space trip.

Pass the sick bag!

Wait for me

No wonder they call it the Vomit Comet!

Do you accept cash?

Gimme a window seat

All aboard!

Most time

Sergei Krikalev has spent more time in Space than anyone else. The Russian made six individual trips between 1988 and 2005, and spent a total of 803.4 days in Space.

Longest stay

The record for the longest single stay in Space is held by Russian Valeri Poliakov. He spent 437.7 days aboard the Mir Space station from 1994–5 when he orbited Earth more than 7,000 times.

First spacewalk

Russia's Alexei Leonov was first to go outside a spacecraft. On 18 March 1965, while secured by a tether to Voskhod 2, he did a ten minute spacewalk. Today, astronauts have made more than 300 walks.

Man on the Moon

On 20 July 1969, US astronaut Neil Armstrong became the first person to walk on the Moon. He famously declared, "That's one small step for man, one giant leap for mankind".

First woman

Russian astronaut Valentina Tereshkova was the first woman in Space when she lifted-off aboard Vostok 6 on 16 June 1963 and orbited Earth 48 times. At least 50 females have been to Space since.

First in Space

The first human into Space was Yuri Gagarin. He travelled once around Earth in Vostok 1 on 12 April 1961. He took off from his own country, Russia, and landed back there 108 minutes later.

Hall of heroes

Most astronauts have travelled only as far as a few hundred kilometres above Earth. Only 26 people have been further; they went to the Moon and back, with 12 of them walking on its surface.

Famous faces

My heroine!

Couldn't put a foot wrong

So long

I'll beat your record...

Space wardrobe

Three types of clothes are needed for a trip into Space. The launch and entry suit is worn for the journey to Space and back, a spacesuit is worn by an astronaut when outside the spacecraft, and casual clothes are worn inside.

I'll give them fashion tips

Spacesuit

The white spacesuit provides an astronaut with their own Earth-like environment. It protects against the temperature extremes of Space, keeps the air pressure around the astronaut's body at the right level, and provides oxygen to breathe.

Launch and entry suit

This one-piece suit with helmet and oxygen system is designed to protect the astronaut in an emergency. A harness with a parachute attached fits over the top.

Everyday wear

Astronauts have a range of casual clothes. Shorts and t-shirts are worn if the inside temperature is high, or they are exercising. Other options include tracksuits, sports shirts, and sweaters.

Rowdy crowd

Great outfit

Supermodel in Space!

Suits you

So next season

Smile, please!

Work that casual catwalk

Keep it casual

Training

Astronaut training usually takes about two years and covers the basics, as well as training for a specific mission. The work includes classroom study, handling Space equipment, and survival techniques in case the returning astronaut lands on a remote part of Earth.

Virtual reality

Trainees become familiar with spacecraft by using virtual reality equipment. A special head set and gloves used with computer displays let them simulate the real movements they would make in Space.

Easy peasy

Where's toilet training?

Spacewalking

A huge water tank is used by astronauts preparing for spacewalks. The underwater conditions simulate the strange feeling of weightlessness as the astronauts practise work routines alongside mock-ups of real spacecraft.

What's up, fish face?

...Who let you in?

Oh my cod!...

Weightlessness

The first taste of real weightlessness comes in a specially modified plane. As the plane flies on the downward part of its path, known as a parabolic loop, anyone inside feels weightless for 25 seconds.

What a feeling!

Take me!

Astronauts wanted

About 500 men and women, from about 40 nations, have left Earth and travelled into Space. These astronauts were selected by Space agencies who trained them for their missions. They were launched by either the USA, Russia, or China. This was the only way to get to Space until 2001, when tourists had the opportunity to make a journey of a lifetime.

Is the pig applying, too?

I'm a lucky swine

We go everywhere together

I'll pass with flying colours

Job application

National Space agencies occasionally advertise for astronauts, though competition is fierce. When European astronauts were recruited in 2008, more than 8,400 people applied. Potential astronauts need outstanding ability in a scientific subject, as well as mental and physical fitness.

Normal weight? Ummm

Mentally sound? Hmmm

Astronaut requirements

Age: 27 to 37 years old

Height: 153–190 cm (60–75 in)

Language: Speak and read English

Education: University degree or equivalent in science-based subject

Health: Good, of normal weight, mentally sound

Personal qualities: Good reasoning, good memory, high motivation, flexibility, emotional stability

Extra assets: Flying experience

Here comes dinner!

Home from home

The ISS provides everything that the astronauts need for everyday life. There is a galley-style kitchen, exercise equipment, and sleeping cabins. Lockers house their personal items, including clothes, books, and toiletries.

The new recruits are settling in!

I'm enjoying my own Space

Space sick

Some astronauts experience Space sickness at the start of a trip. The headache and vomiting last only a day or two, but puffy eyes, a stuffy nose, and a slow heartbeat, which are the result of gravity not pulling on the body, affect everyone and last throughout the stay.

Great to be back!

Space Station

The ISS consists of 18 major parts, launched separately and assembled in Space. The first parts were fitted together in 1998, and the station is almost complete. It is about the size of a football pitch, and inside has the space of a five-bedroom house.

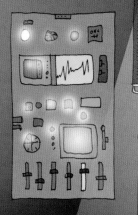

What on Earth is going on?
Let me tell you...

Solar panels on each side of the orbiter convert the Sun's energy to electrical power

Crew on board

Astronauts have lived on the station since the first three-person crew moved in on 2 November 2000 and stayed for 138 days. Crews consist of up to six astronauts at a time and include men and women from different nations.

Get on board!

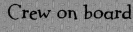

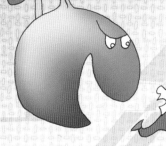

Wowsers!

That's one hungry hopper!

LiVING iN SPACE

Astronauts live on board the International Space Station (ISS) about 390 km (240 miles) above Earth. This home and workplace orbits around our planet at 28,000 kph (17,500 mph), completing one circuit every 90 minutes. Astronauts are transported to and from the ISS by spacecraft that dock temporarily at the station. Days are spent building and maintaining the station, as well as carrying out scientific investigations. Crews usually stay for several months at a time.

Am I dreaming?
Stop snoring
We've got a floater!

Sleep tight

After a 16-hour working day, astronauts are ready for their eight hours of sleep. Their sleeping bags are fixed down so they do not float around. An eye-mask and ear plugs block out the light and noise of the station.

Keeping in shape

The astronauts follow an exercise routine for two hours a day to stay fit and healthy. The treadmill and bike not only exercise their muscles but also counteract the loss of calcium from their bones, as a result of the weightless conditions.

Mealtime

Favourite foods are chosen by astronauts before their departure and are incorporated into menus on a ten-day cycle. They have three meals a day, as well as extra snacks and drinks. The prepared and packaged food is re-hydrated and heated as needed.

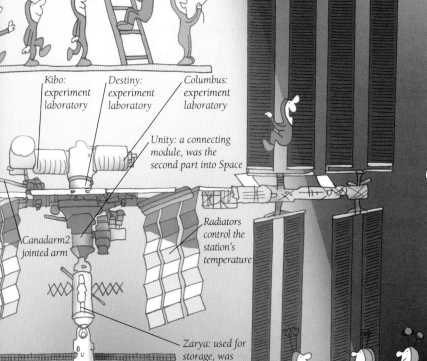

Kibo: experiment laboratory

Destiny: experiment laboratory

Columbus: experiment laboratory

Unity: a connecting module, was the second part into Space

Canadarm2 jointed arm

Radiators control the station's temperature

Zarya: used for storage, was the first part into Space

Zvezda: includes the crew's living area

Space work

Weekdays are a routine of experiments and planning. Astronauts work in one of three laboratories – Destiny, Columbus, or Kibo. Experiments include testing their own bodies to learn how they are affected by Space. The results will help in the planning of future missions.

Spacewalk

Astronauts have made more than 120 spacewalks to install new parts of the station and carry out repairs. An individual is anchored to Canadarm2, a 17.6-m (55-ft) jointed arm that can move the full length of the station as they work.

Personal hygiene

Astronauts keep clean by having a daily sponge bath. There are two cloths each – one for washing and one for rinsing. They use one of the two toilets on board the station and clean their hair with rinse-less shampoo.

Spare time

At weekends, astronauts do household chores and relax. A favourite pastime is looking out of the window, but they also read, play games, take photographs, listen to music, watch films, and have races in the station.

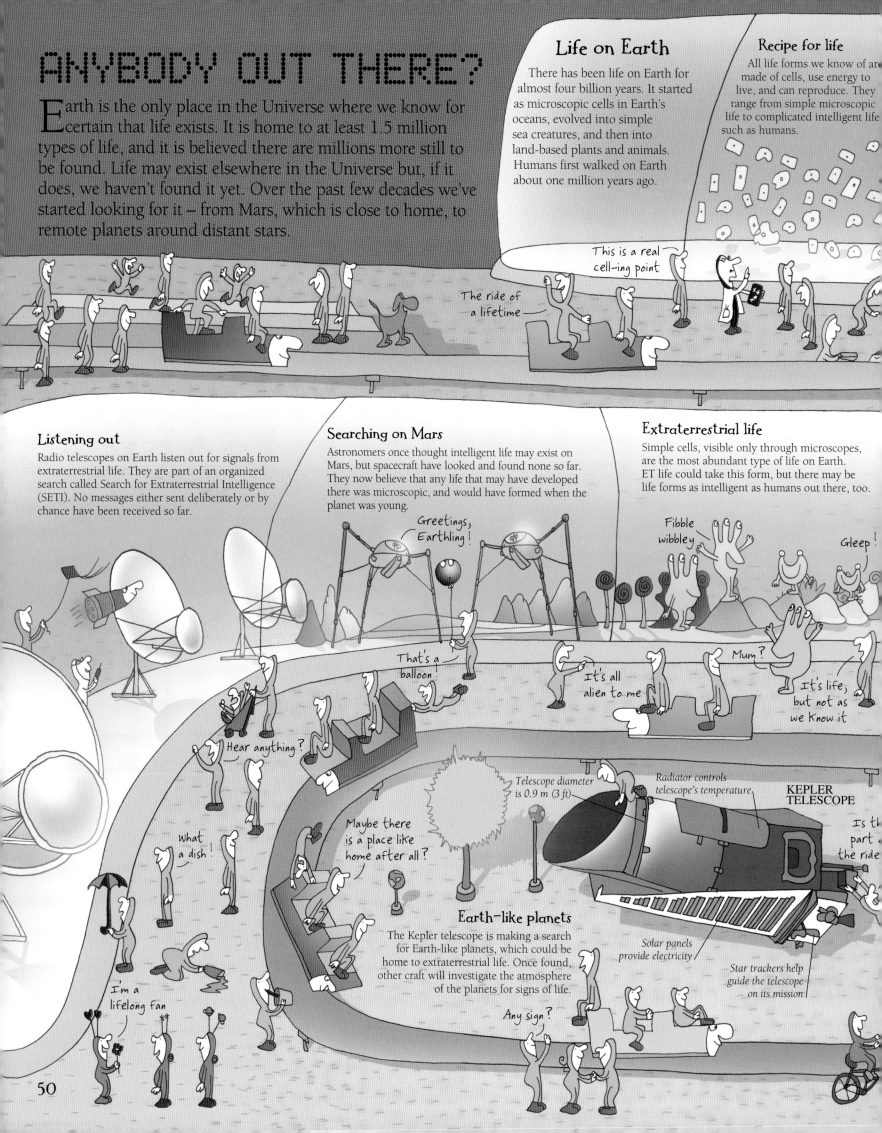

ANYBODY OUT THERE?

Earth is the only place in the Universe where we know for certain that life exists. It is home to at least 1.5 million types of life, and it is believed there are millions more still to be found. Life may exist elsewhere in the Universe but, if it does, we haven't found it yet. Over the past few decades we've started looking for it – from Mars, which is close to home, to remote planets around distant stars.

Life on Earth

There has been life on Earth for almost four billion years. It started as microscopic cells in Earth's oceans, evolved into simple sea creatures, and then into land-based plants and animals. Humans first walked on Earth about one million years ago.

Recipe for life

All life forms we know of are made of cells, use energy to live, and can reproduce. They range from simple microscopic life to complicated intelligent life such as humans.

Listening out

Radio telescopes on Earth listen out for signals from extraterrestrial life. They are part of an organized search called Search for Extraterrestrial Intelligence (SETI). No messages either sent deliberately or by chance have been received so far.

Searching on Mars

Astronomers once thought intelligent life may exist on Mars, but spacecraft have looked and found none so far. They now believe that any life that may have developed there was microscopic, and would have formed when the planet was young.

Extraterrestrial life

Simple cells, visible only through microscopes, are the most abundant type of life on Earth. ET life could take this form, but there may be life forms as intelligent as humans out there, too.

Earth-like planets

The Kepler telescope is making a search for Earth-like planets, which could be home to extraterrestrial life. Once found, other craft will investigate the atmosphere of the planets for signs of life.

Telescope diameter is 0.9 m (3 ft)

Radiator controls telescope's temperature

KEPLER TELESCOPE

Solar panels provide electricity

Star trackers help guide the telescope on its mission

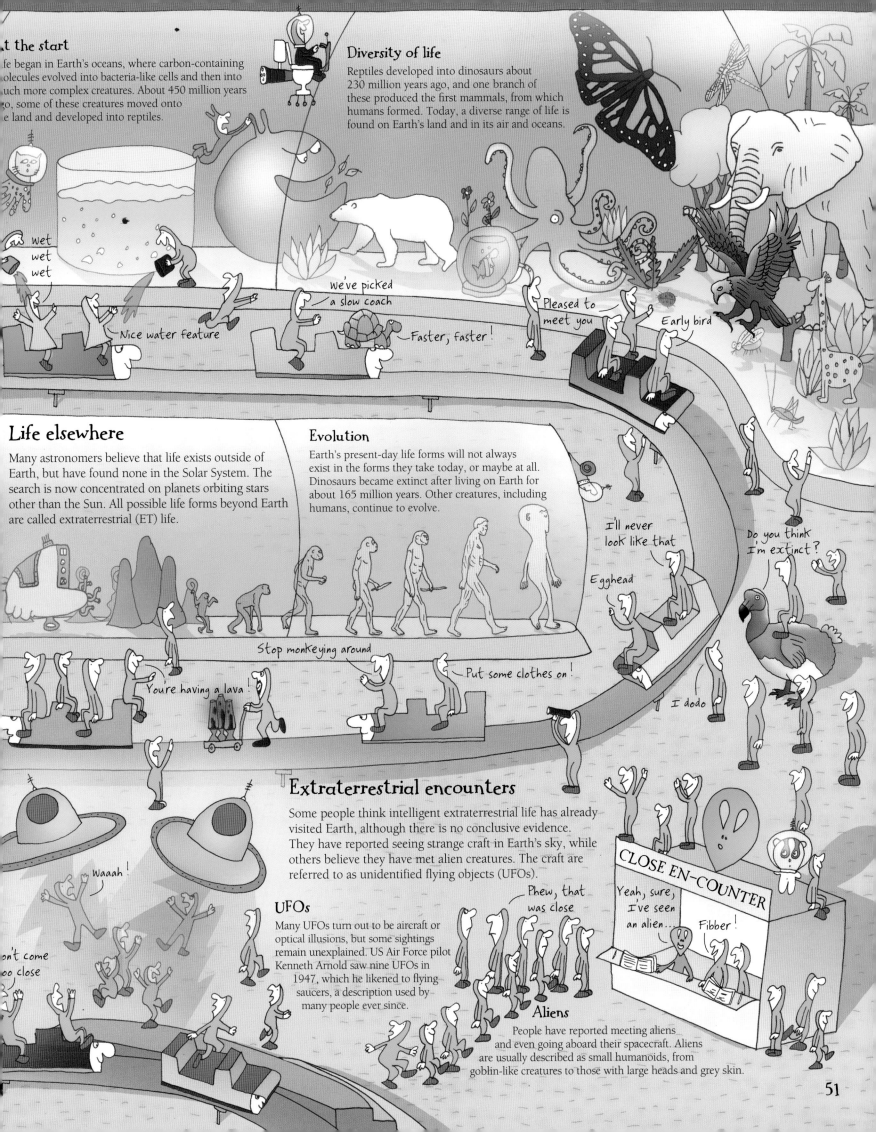

At the start

Life began in Earth's oceans, where carbon-containing molecules evolved into bacteria-like cells and then into much more complex creatures. About 450 million years ago, some of these creatures moved onto the land and developed into reptiles.

Diversity of life

Reptiles developed into dinosaurs about 230 million years ago, and one branch of these produced the first mammals, from which humans formed. Today, a diverse range of life is found on Earth's land and in its air and oceans.

Life elsewhere

Many astronomers believe that life exists outside of Earth, but have found none in the Solar System. The search is now concentrated on planets orbiting stars other than the Sun. All possible life forms beyond Earth are called extraterrestrial (ET) life.

Evolution

Earth's present-day life forms will not always exist in the forms they take today, or maybe at all. Dinosaurs became extinct after living on Earth for about 165 million years. Other creatures, including humans, continue to evolve.

Extraterrestrial encounters

Some people think intelligent extraterrestrial life has already visited Earth, although there is no conclusive evidence. They have reported seeing strange craft in Earth's sky, while others believe they have met alien creatures. The craft are referred to as unidentified flying objects (UFOs).

UFOs

Many UFOs turn out to be aircraft or optical illusions, but some sightings remain unexplained. US Air Force pilot Kenneth Arnold saw nine UFOs in 1947, which he likened to flying saucers, a description used by many people ever since.

Aliens

People have reported meeting aliens and even going aboard their spacecraft. Aliens are usually described as small humanoids, from goblin-like creatures to those with large heads and grey skin.

51

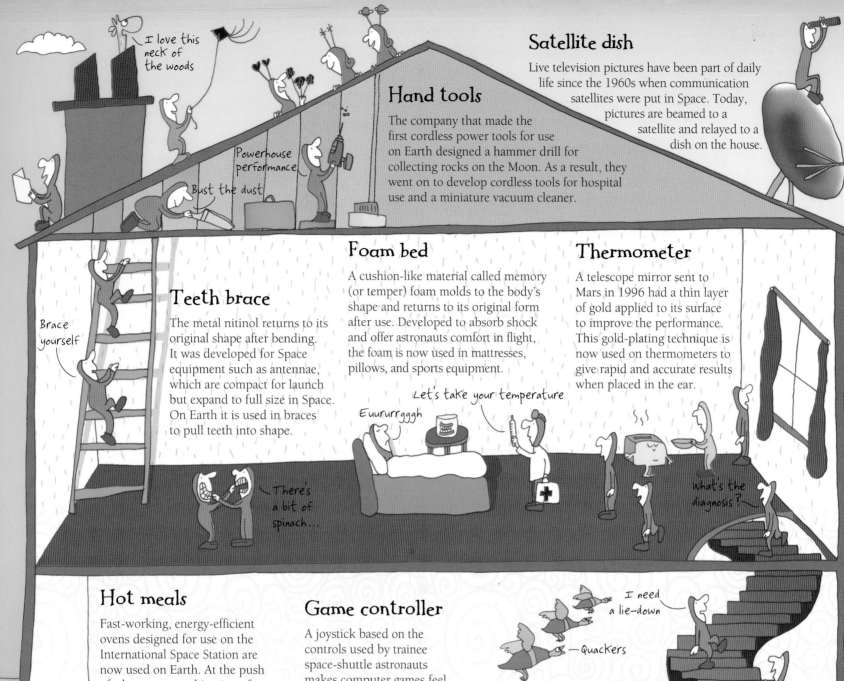

Satellite dish

Live television pictures have been part of daily life since the 1960s when communication satellites were put in Space. Today, pictures are beamed to a satellite and relayed to a dish on the house.

Hand tools

The company that made the first cordless power tools for use on Earth designed a hammer drill for collecting rocks on the Moon. As a result, they went on to develop cordless tools for hospital use and a miniature vacuum cleaner.

Teeth brace

The metal nitinol returns to its original shape after bending. It was developed for Space equipment such as antennae, which are compact for launch but expand to full size in Space. On Earth it is used in braces to pull teeth into shape.

Foam bed

A cushion-like material called memory (or temper) foam molds to the body's shape and returns to its original form after use. Developed to absorb shock and offer astronauts comfort in flight, the foam is now used in mattresses, pillows, and sports equipment.

Thermometer

A telescope mirror sent to Mars in 1996 had a thin layer of gold applied to its surface to improve the performance. This gold-plating technique is now used on thermometers to give rapid and accurate results when placed in the ear.

Hot meals

Fast-working, energy-efficient ovens designed for use on the International Space Station are now used on Earth. At the push of a button, a combination of microwaves and jets of hot air heat the food rapidly.

Game controller

A joystick based on the controls used by trainee space-shuttle astronauts makes computer games feel more real. The hand grip replicates all three movements (pitch, roll, and yaw) of the shuttle and also includes the throttle control.

Water filter

Astronauts need clear, safe, and good-tasting water. A pocket-sized water filter that removes unwanted substances was developed for the Apollo spacecraft. It has been adapted for use in the home.

Space spin-offs

The Space industry affects everyone's lives, even though they may not know it. Materials, equipment, and techniques designed for use in Space are used regularly on Earth. Sometimes the transfer of the technology is direct, but often it is adapted to an area unrelated to the original use. The benefits of the Space industry are enjoyed every day by all of us.

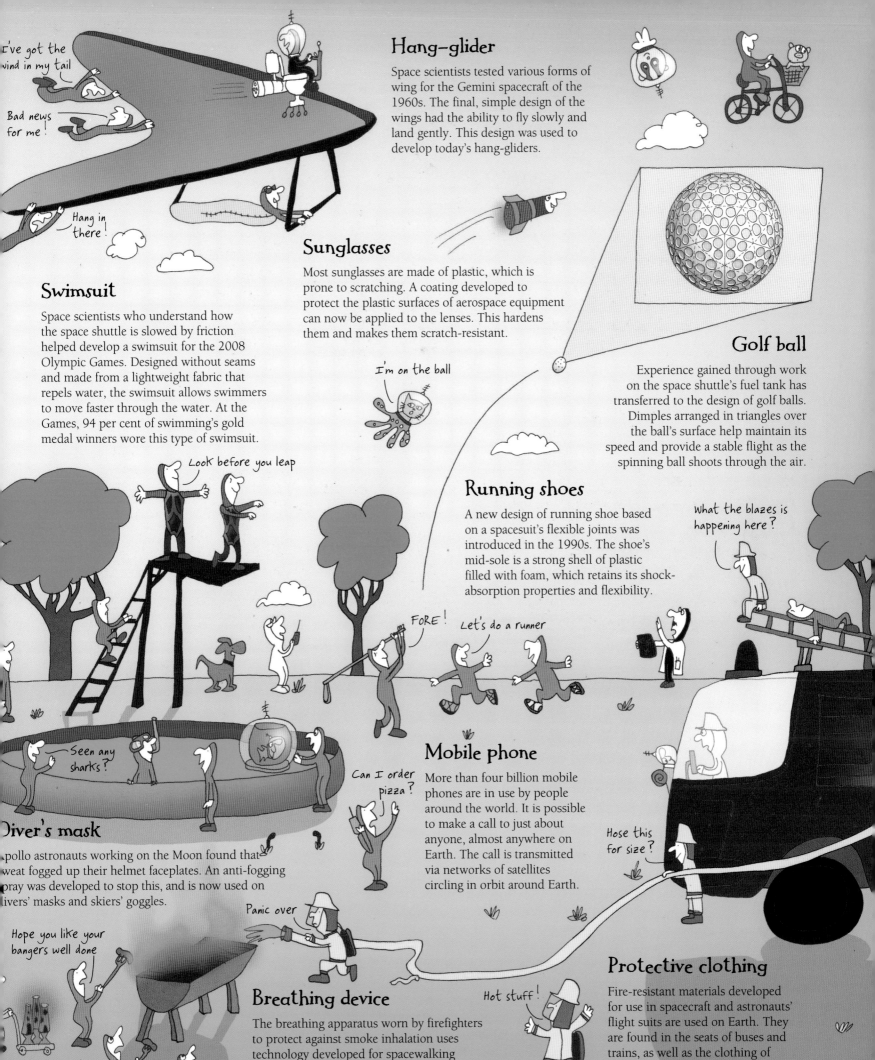

Hang-glider

Space scientists tested various forms of wing for the Gemini spacecraft of the 1960s. The final, simple design of the wings had the ability to fly slowly and land gently. This design was used to develop today's hang-gliders.

Sunglasses

Most sunglasses are made of plastic, which is prone to scratching. A coating developed to protect the plastic surfaces of aerospace equipment can now be applied to the lenses. This hardens them and makes them scratch-resistant.

Swimsuit

Space scientists who understand how the space shuttle is slowed by friction helped develop a swimsuit for the 2008 Olympic Games. Designed without seams and made from a lightweight fabric that repels water, the swimsuit allows swimmers to move faster through the water. At the Games, 94 per cent of swimming's gold medal winners wore this type of swimsuit.

Golf ball

Experience gained through work on the space shuttle's fuel tank has transferred to the design of golf balls. Dimples arranged in triangles over the ball's surface help maintain its speed and provide a stable flight as the spinning ball shoots through the air.

Running shoes

A new design of running shoe based on a spacesuit's flexible joints was introduced in the 1990s. The shoe's mid-sole is a strong shell of plastic filled with foam, which retains its shock-absorption properties and flexibility.

Mobile phone

More than four billion mobile phones are in use by people around the world. It is possible to make a call to just about anyone, almost anywhere on Earth. The call is transmitted via networks of satellites circling in orbit around Earth.

Diver's mask

Apollo astronauts working on the Moon found that sweat fogged up their helmet faceplates. An anti-fogging spray was developed to stop this, and is now used on divers' masks and skiers' goggles.

Breathing device

The breathing apparatus worn by firefighters to protect against smoke inhalation uses technology developed for spacewalking astronauts. It is lightweight and easy to wear, while the face mask gives clear vision.

Protective clothing

Fire-resistant materials developed for use in spacecraft and astronauts' flight suits are used on Earth. They are found in the seats of buses and trains, as well as the clothing of racing drivers and firefighters.

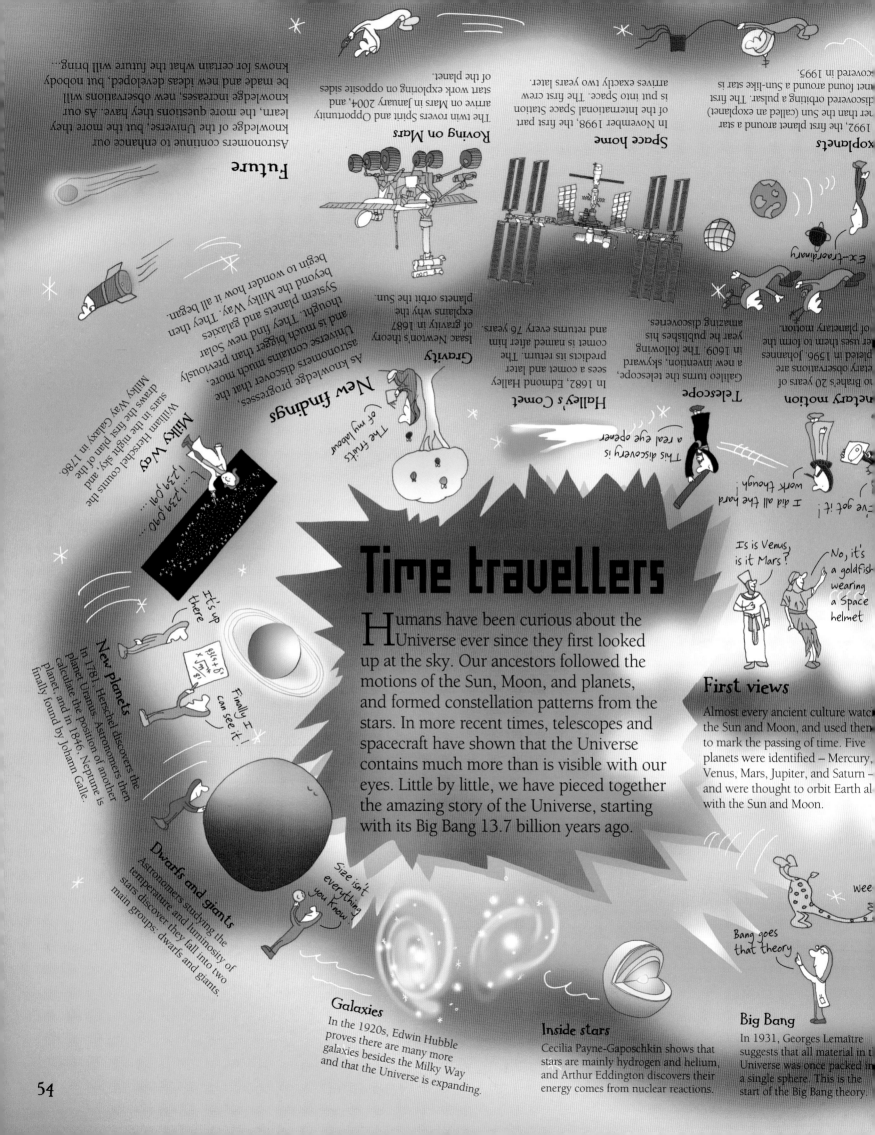

Time travellers

Humans have been curious about the Universe ever since they first looked up at the sky. Our ancestors followed the motions of the Sun, Moon, and planets, and formed constellation patterns from the stars. In more recent times, telescopes and spacecraft have shown that the Universe contains much more than is visible with our eyes. Little by little, we have pieced together the amazing story of the Universe, starting with its Big Bang 13.7 billion years ago.

First views

Almost every ancient culture watch[ed] the Sun and Moon, and used them to mark the passing of time. Five planets were identified – Mercury, Venus, Mars, Jupiter, and Saturn – and were thought to orbit Earth al[ong] with the Sun and Moon.

Big Bang

In 1931, Georges Lemaître suggests that all material in th[e] Universe was once packed int[o] a single sphere. This is the start of the Big Bang theory.

Inside stars

Cecilia Payne-Gaposchkin shows that stars are mainly hydrogen and helium, and Arthur Eddington discovers their energy comes from nuclear reactions.

Galaxies

In the 1920s, Edwin Hubble proves there are many more galaxies besides the Milky Way and that the Universe is expanding.

Dwarfs and giants

Astronomers studying the temperature and luminosity of stars discover they fall into two main groups: dwarfs and giants.

New planets

In 1781, Herschel discovers the planet Uranus. Astronomers then calculate the position of another planet, and in 1846, Neptune is finally found by Johann Galle.

Milky Way

William Herschel counts the stars in the night sky, and draws the first plan of the Milky Way Galaxy in 1786.

New findings

As knowledge progresses, astronomers discover that the Universe contains much more. They find new Solar System planets and galaxies beyond the Milky Way. They then begin to wonder how it all began.

Future

Astronomers continue to enhance our knowledge of the Universe, but the more they learn, the more questions they have. As our knowledge increases, new observations will be made and new ideas developed, but nobody knows for certain what the future will bring...

Roving on Mars

The twin rovers Spirit and Opportunity arrive on Mars in January 2004, and start work exploring on opposite sides of the planet.

Space home

In November 1998, the first part of the International Space Station is put into Space. The first crew arrives exactly two years later.

Exoplanets

In 1992, the first planet around a star other than the Sun (called an exoplanet) [is] discovered orbiting a pulsar. The first planet found around a Sun-like star is [di]scovered in 1995.

Planetary motion

[Tych]o Brahe's 20 years of planetary observations are completed in 1596. Johannes [Kepler] uses them to form the [laws] of planetary motion.

Telescope

Galileo turns the telescope, a new invention, skyward in 1609. The following year he publishes his amazing discoveries.

Halley's Comet

In 1682, Edmond Halley sees a comet and later predicts its return. The comet is named after him and returns every 76 years.

Gravity

Isaac Newton's theory of gravity in 1687 explains why the planets orbit the Sun.

Space Telescope

In April 1990, the Hubble Space Telescope is put into orbit around Earth to study the Milky Way stars and galaxies far beyond.

Recent years

More powerful telescopes are used on Earth and in Space to make new discoveries, including planets orbiting stars other than the Sun. Sophisticated robotic craft explore Solar System objects, and astronauts build a home and workplace above Earth.

I'm ready for my close-up.

Space shuttle

On 12 April 1981, exactly 20 years after the first human went into orbit, the first reusable Space vehicle, the space shuttle, is launched.

Space Voyagers

In 1977, the twin spacecraft Voyager 1 and Voyager 2 are launched on missions to the giant planets.

Universal thought

You're the centre of my world

Sun-centred

In 1543, Nicolaus Copernicus publishes his idea that Earth and the other planets move around the Sun. This marks the end of the idea of an Earth-centred Universe.

I'm a clever Nick

Astronomers realise that the Sun is at the centre of the known Universe, and is orbited by the other planets. The newly-invented telescope offers proof, and also reveals there is much more to the Universe.

Aztec calendar

The Sun stone is completed in 1479, containing the calendar system of the Aztec people of Central America.

Chinese observatory

The building of the Beijing observatory in China is finished in 1442. It is one of the great pre-telescopic observatories.

Planet positions

The Alphonsine Tables, which list accurate positions of the Sun, Moon, and planets, are drawn up by scholars working for King Alphonso X of Spain in 1252.

Yes King Alphonso!

No slacking!

Black hole

In the 1970s, Cygnus X-1 is identified as the first black hole, but it is several years before all astronomers are convinced.

Bright spark

See, they're spherical!

I can't get my head a-round this idea

My stars!

r patterns

about 4000 BCE, Egyptians, Chaldeans, Hindus had named bright stars and formed n into constellations.

Spherical worlds

In about 550 BCE, the Greek mathematician Pythagoras suggests the Sun, Moon, Earth, and planets are all spherical.

Earth-centred

Hipparchus produces a catalogue of stars in about 200 BCE, and Ptolemy later refines the idea that Earth is at the centre of the Universe.

Middle Ages

People continue to believe in the Earth-centred Universe, an idea developed by the Ancient Greeks and passed on by Arab scholars. More accurate observations are made of the planets as they move across the sky, and eclipses, comets, and new stars are all noted.

This is such a buzz!

Moon landing

On 20 July 1969, Neil Armstrong becomes the first human to walk on another world when he steps onto the Moon. Buzz Aldrin is the second.

Sidney, you'll make yourself ill!

I'm numero uno

First to Space

Yuri Gagarin becomes the first human in Space on 12 April 1961. He takes 108 minutes to travel once around Earth.

Space Age

Astronomers keep studying the nature of the stars and galaxies. Telescopes are launched into Space around Earth, and robotic craft are sent to explore Solar System objects. The first astronauts travel into Space – starting near Earth, but later going to the Moon.

Sputnik 1

The first spacecraft, the satellite Sputnik 1, is put into orbit around Earth in 1957. The Space Age has begun.

FUTURE SPACE

The more we learn about the Universe, the more fascinating it becomes. There are always new questions to be answered and new places to go. In the years ahead, increasingly powerful telescopes will look further into Space, robotic craft will embark on new missions, and astronauts will once again step on the Moon and also travel to a new destination, Mars. In the future, people will have the chance to launch off from Earth and experience Space for themselves.

JAMES WEBB SPACE TELESCOPE

Main mirror is 6.5 m (21 ft) in width

Sunshield, the size of a tennis court, helps keep the telescope cool

Telescopes

Positioned in Space, the James Webb Space Telescope will study the infrared Universe from 2013. This is the successor to the Hubble Space Telescope. On Earth, the Giant Magellan Telescope in Chile will be the biggest to date. Scheduled for completion in 2018, its main mirror, which is a set of smaller mirrors working together, is 24 m (80 ft) in width.

ORION

Orion's crew module holds up to six astronauts

Service module provides propulsion and power

Return to the Moon

The Orion craft will take over the space shuttle's role of carrying crew to the International Space Station from 2014. At a future date it will transport astronauts to and from the Moon. A separate surface module will undock from Orion and deliver the crew to the lunar surface.

Surface module carries astronauts between Orion and lunar surface

Living on the Moon

Astronauts will stay on the Moon for up to six months at a time before returning home in Orion. A living module will be their base for daily exploration of the lunar surface. Rovers will transport them to distant locations.

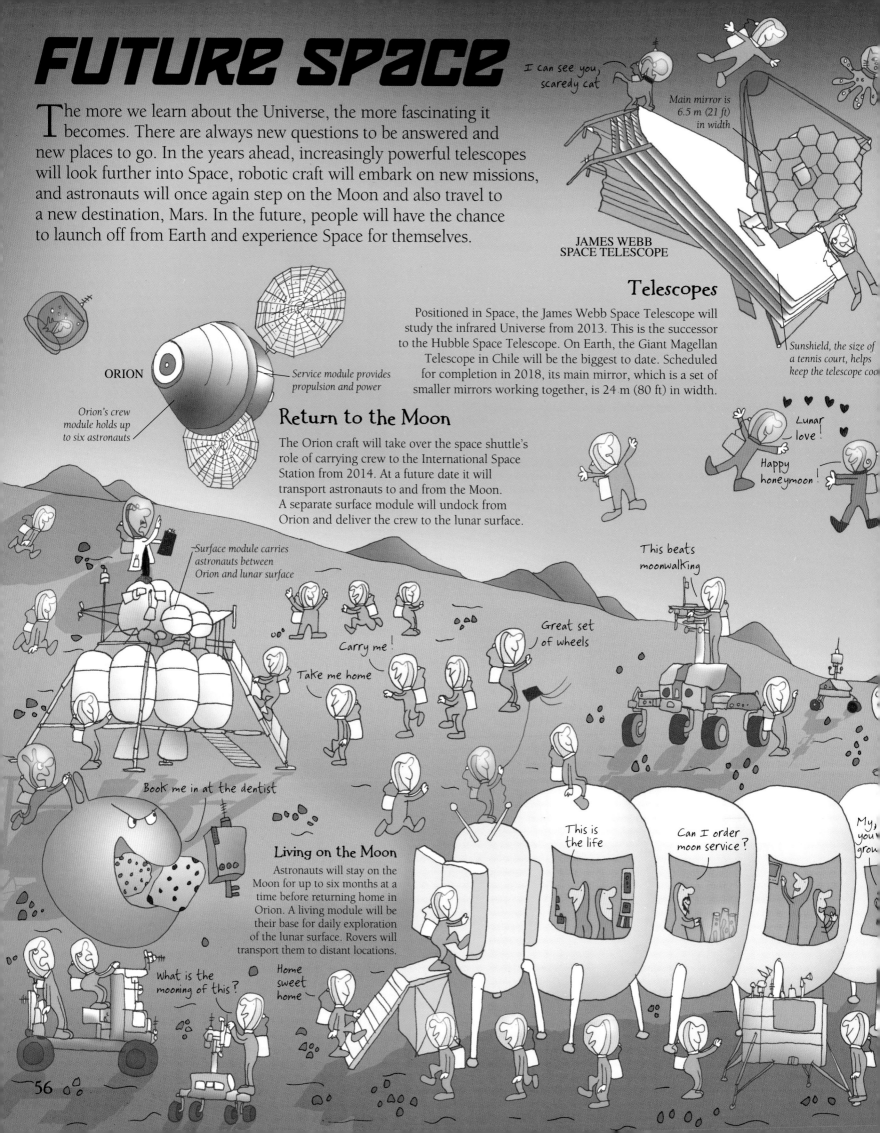

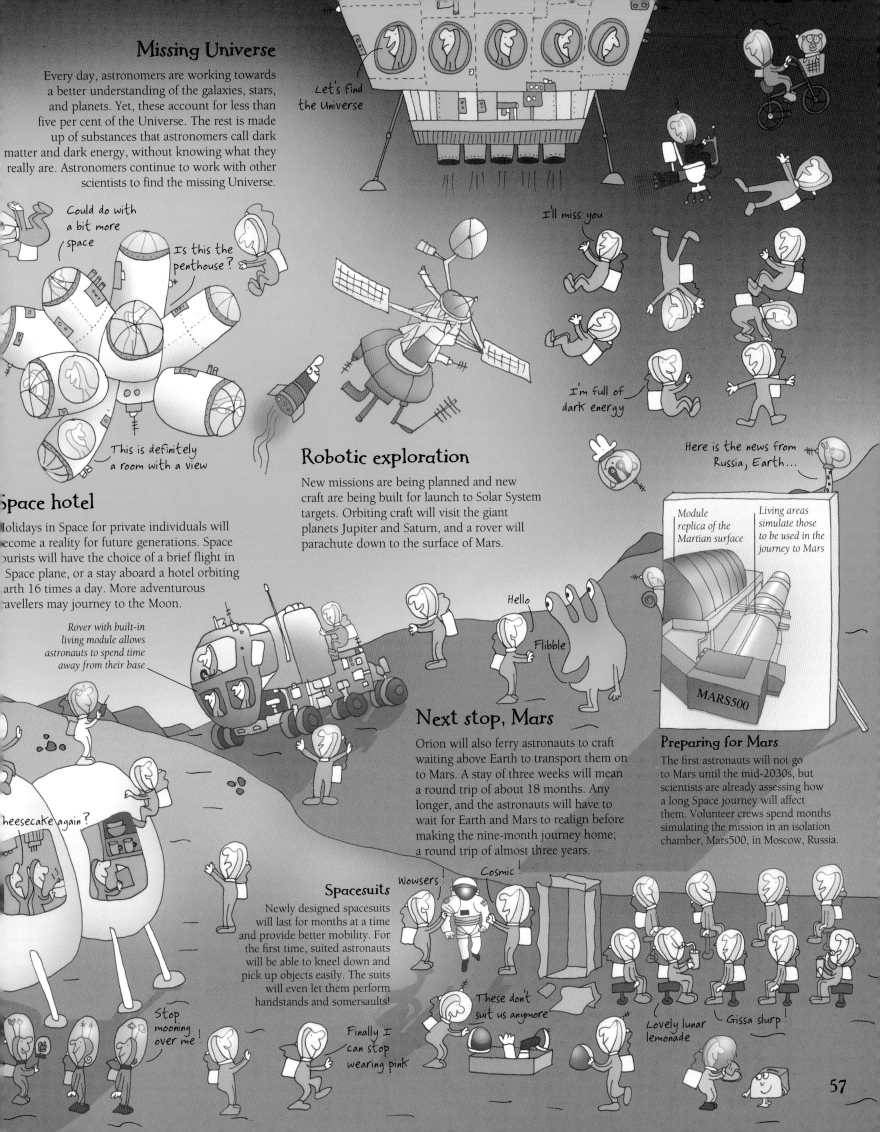

Missing Universe

Every day, astronomers are working towards a better understanding of the galaxies, stars, and planets. Yet, these account for less than five per cent of the Universe. The rest is made up of substances that astronomers call dark matter and dark energy, without knowing what they really are. Astronomers continue to work with other scientists to find the missing Universe.

Space hotel

Holidays in Space for private individuals will become a reality for future generations. Space tourists will have the choice of a brief flight in a Space plane, or a stay aboard a hotel orbiting Earth 16 times a day. More adventurous travellers may journey to the Moon.

Rover with built-in living module allows astronauts to spend time away from their base

Robotic exploration

New missions are being planned and new craft are being built for launch to Solar System targets. Orbiting craft will visit the giant planets Jupiter and Saturn, and a rover will parachute down to the surface of Mars.

Next stop, Mars

Orion will also ferry astronauts to craft waiting above Earth to transport them on to Mars. A stay of three weeks will mean a round trip of about 18 months. Any longer, and the astronauts will have to wait for Earth and Mars to realign before making the nine-month journey home; a round trip of almost three years.

Spacesuits

Newly designed spacesuits will last for months at a time and provide better mobility. For the first time, suited astronauts will be able to kneel down and pick up objects easily. The suits will even let them perform handstands and somersaults!

Module replica of the Martian surface

Living areas simulate those to be used in the journey to Mars

MARS500

Preparing for Mars

The first astronauts will not go to Mars until the mid-2030s, but scientists are already assessing how a long Space journey will affect them. Volunteer crews spend months simulating the mission in an isolation chamber, Mars500, in Moscow, Russia.

GLOSSARY

Active galaxy
A galaxy that emits an exceptional amount of energy, much of which comes from a supermassive black hole in its centre.

Alien
A creature that originates from a world other than Earth.

Antenna
An aerial in the shape of a rod, dish, or array for receiving or transmitting radio waves.

Apparent magnitude
A measure of the apparent brightness of a star when seen from Earth.

Asteroid
A small rocky body orbiting the Sun. Most are in the Main Belt between Mars and Jupiter.

Astronaut
A man or woman who travels into Space.

Astronomer
Someone who studies stars, planets, and other objects in Space.

Atmosphere
The layer of gases held around a planet, moon, or star by its gravity.

Atom
The smallest piece of a chemical element.

Aurora
A light display over a planet's polar regions produced when particles hit atoms in the planet's atmosphere, making the atmosphere glow.

Big Bang
The explosive event that created the Universe 13.7 billion years ago.

Black hole
A star or galaxy core that has collapsed in on itself. Black holes have gravity so strong that no matter, light, or other radiation can escape from them.

Brightness
A measure of the light of a star. Astronomers measure brightness in two ways: as seen from Earth, and the amount of light a star emits.

Cell
The basic unit in all living things. A cell may exist as an independent unit of life, or many can combine to form complex tissue, as in plants and animals.

Cluster
A group of galaxies or stars held together by gravity.

Comet
A small snow and dust body. Those travelling near the Sun develop a huge head and two tails.

Constellation
An imaginary pattern of stars and the region of sky around them. Earth's sky is divided into 88 different constellations.

Convection
The transfer of heat by movement, for example, when warmer gas rises and cooler gas falls in a star.

Cosmologist
A person who studies the origin, evolution, and future of the Universe.

Crater
A bowl-shaped hollow on the surface of a planet or moon formed when an asteroid crashes into it.

Dark energy
A mysterious energy form that makes up 72 per cent of the Universe and is responsible for the acceleration of the expansion of the Universe.

Dark matter
Matter that does not emit energy but whose gravity affects its surroundings. It makes up 23 per cent of the Universe.

Density
A measure of how tightly the mass an object possesses is packed into its volume.

Dwarf galaxy
A small galaxy containing only a million to several billion stars.

Dwarf planet
An almost round body that orbits the Sun as part of a belt of objects.

Eclipse
The effect achieved when a body, such as a star, planet, or moon, is in the shadow of another.

Electromagnetic radiation
A range of energy waves that can travel through Space. They include gamma rays, X-rays, ultraviolet, light, infrared, microwaves, and radio waves.

Element
A basic substance of nature, such as hydrogen or oxygen.

Elliptical
Something shaped like an elongated circle.

Equator
An imaginary line drawn around the middle of a planet, moon, or star, halfway between its north and south poles.

Exoplanet
A planet that orbits a star other than the Sun. Sometimes called an extrasolar planet.

Extraterrestrial
Something or somebody that comes from somewhere other than Earth.

Fly-by
A close encounter made with a Solar System object by a spacecraft, which flies past without going into orbit.

Galaxy
An enormous grouping of stars, gas, and dust held together by gravity.

Giant planets
The four largest Solar System planets. In order of decreasing size and distance from the Sun, they are Jupiter, Saturn, Uranus, and Neptune.

Gravity
A force of attraction found throughout the Universe. The greater the mass of a body, the greater its gravitational pull.

Helium
The second most abundant chemical element in the Universe.

Hydrogen
The lightest and most abundant chemical element in the Universe.

Kuiper Belt Object
A rock and ice body orbiting the Sun within the Kuiper Belt, beyond the orbit of Neptune.

Lander
A spacecraft that lands on the surface of a planet, moon, asteroid, or comet.

Lava
Molten rock released through a volcano on the surface of a planet or moon.

Light year
A unit of distance. One light year (ly) is the distance light travels in one year, which is 9.46 million million km (5.88 million million miles).

Luminosity
The total amount of energy emitted in one second by a star.

Lunar
Relating to the Moon. For example, the "lunar surface" is the surface of the Moon.

Magnetic field
Any place where a magnetic force can be measured, such as around Earth.

Main sequence
A stage in the lifetime of a star when the star shines by converting hydrogen into helium in its core. About 90 per cent of stars are main sequence stars.

Mare
A smooth plain of solidified lava on the Moon. (pl. maria)

Mass
A measure of the amount of material (matter) a body is made of.

Matter
The substance that things are made of.

Meteor
A short-lived streak of light produced by a small piece of a comet burning up in Earth's upper atmosphere.

Get off my toaster!

It's a race to the finish

Meteorite
Rock or metal from Space that lands on the surface of a planet or moon.

Milky Way
The galaxy we live in. Also, the name given to the band of stars that crosses Earth's sky and which is our view into the galaxy.

Module
A complete unit of a spacecraft, for instance, the Zvezda module of the International Space Station.

Moon
A rock or rock-and-ice body, that orbits a planet or an asteroid.

Nebula
A cloud of gas and dust in Space. Some nebulae emit their own light, others shine by reflecting light, and those that block out light from background stars appear dark.

Neutron star
A dense, compact star formed from the core of an exploding star. These stars are about the size of a city but have the same mass as the Sun.

Nuclear reaction
The process whereby elements inside a star produce other elements and energy is released. For example, hydrogen atoms fuse to produce helium, and energy such as heat and light is emitted in the process.

Nucleus
The body of a comet, the central part of a galaxy, or the central core of an atom. (pl. nuclei)

Oort Cloud
A sphere consisting of more than a trillion comets that surrounds the planetary part of the Solar System.

Orbit
The path that a natural or artificial body makes around another more massive body.

Orbiter
A spacecraft that orbits around a Space body such as a planet or asteroid.

Organism
An individual form of life such as a single-celled bacterium, an animal, or a plant.

Penumbra
The lighter, outer part of a shadow cast by a Space body. Also, the lighter and warmer outer region of a dark, cool sunspot.

Photosphere
The outer, visible layer of the Sun or another star.

Planet
A massive, round body that orbits a star and shines by reflecting the star's light.

Planetary nebula
An expanding nebula surrounding a mature star. This nebula is a colourful cloud of ejected gas and dust from the dying star.

Polar
Relating to the North and South Poles of an object.

Pressure
The force felt when something presses against a surface.

Protostar
A very young star in the early stages of formation, before nuclear reactions start in its core.

Pulsar
A rapidly rotating neutron star from which brief pulses of energy are received as the star spins.

Radiation
Energy travelling as electromagnetic waves such as infrared or light.

Rocky planets
The four planets closest to the Sun and made of rock and/or metal. They are Mercury, Venus, Earth, and Mars.

Rover
A spacecraft that moves across the surface of a planet or moon.

Satellite
An artificial object put deliberately in orbit around Earth, or another Solar System body. Also, another name for a moon, or any Space object orbiting a much larger one.

Silicate
Rocky material containing the elements silicon, oxygen, and one or more other common elements. Most rocks on Earth are silicates.

Solar
Relating to the Sun. For example, the "solar temperature" is the temperature of the Sun.

Solar nebula
The spinning cloud of gas and dust that formed into the Solar System.

Solar System
The Sun and the objects that orbit it, including the planets and many smaller bodies.

Solar wind
A stream of particles emitted by the Sun.

Spacesuit
The all-in-one sealed clothing unit worn by astronauts when outside their craft in Space.

Spacewalk
An excursion by an astronaut outside a craft when in Space.

Spectrograph
An instrument that splits energy, such as light, into its component wavelengths. This is then analysed to reveal an object's properties.

Spectrum
The rainbow band of colours that is produced when light is split.

Star
A huge sphere of hot, luminous gas that generates energy by nuclear reactions.

Supercluster
A grouping of galaxy clusters held together by gravity.

Supergiant
An exceptionally large and luminous star.

Supernova
A massive star that explodes and leaves material behind, and whose core can become a neutron star, pulsar, or black hole. (pl. supernovae)

Thermal
Relating to heat. A thermal map of an object shows the temperature across the surface of that object.

Umbra
The dark, inner shadow cast by a Space body. Also, the darker, cooler inner region of a sunspot.

Universe
Everything that exists – Space and everything in it.

Vacuum
A space that is void of matter, including air.

Volume
The amount of space an object occupies.

Wavelength
The distance between the peaks or troughs in waves of energy.

Weightlessness
The sensation experienced by astronauts in Space because being in orbit is like constantly falling through Space.

Zodiac
The band of 12 constellations that forms the background to the Sun, Moon, and planets as they move across the sky.

What's that strange rumbling noise?

This is stellar stuff!

INDEX

That's where my cheese got to

Sidney'll need my pump

He won't be hopping for a while

Acknowledgements

Dorling Kindersley would like to thank Stephanie Pliakas for proofreading, Jackie Brind for the index, and Jenny Finch for naming Sidney Spacehopper.

No Brainwaves were harmed during the making of this book.

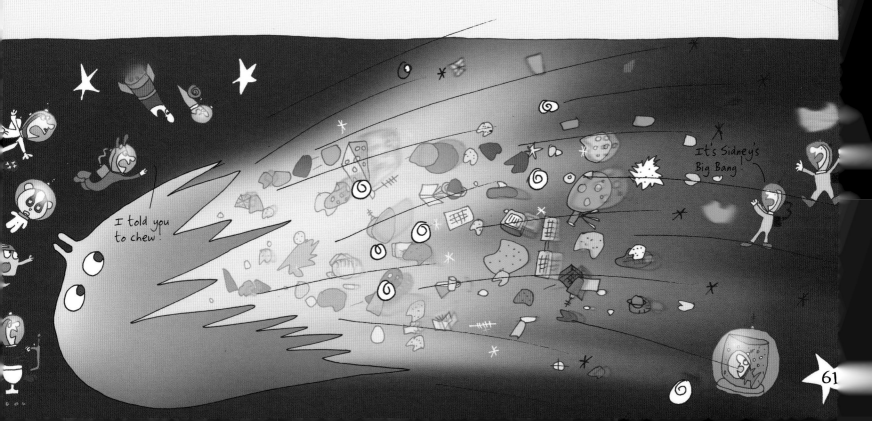

I told you to chew!

It's Sidney's Big Bang

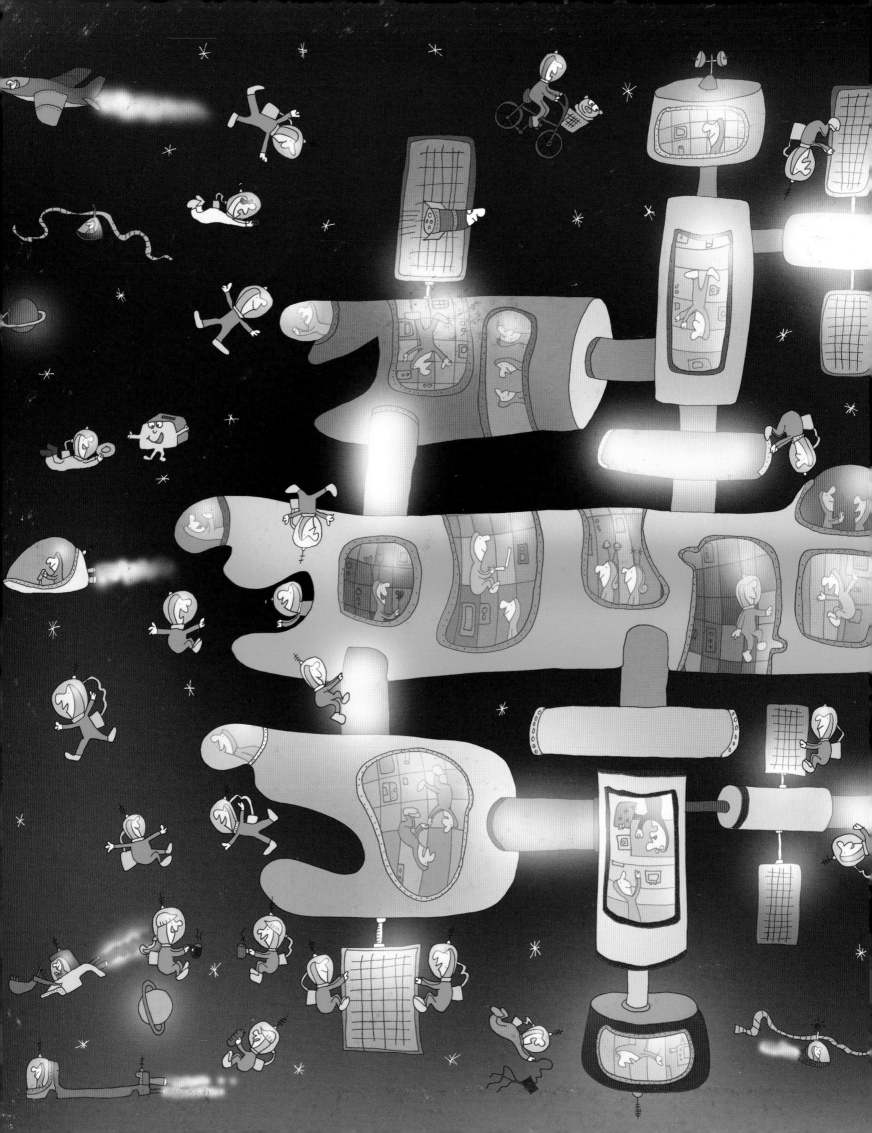